THE
Modern Mom's
MEMORY JOURNAL

Inspired Prompts for the Good, the Gross, the Messy, and the Magical

Adamsmedia
Avon, Massachusetts

Published by
Adams Media, a division of F+W Media, Inc.
57 Littlefield Street, Avon, MA 02322. U.S.A.
www.adamsmedia.com

ISBN 10: 1-4405-6104-4
ISBN 13: 978-1-4405-6104-7

Printed in the United States of America.

10   9   8   7   6   5   4   3   2

*This book is available at quantity discounts for bulk purchases.
For information, please call 1-800-289-0963.*

INTRODUCTION

Real Memories for Real Moms

You'll never forget your child's first words or first steps. But being a mom is about so much more than those big, watershed moments.

Every day, your child amazes you.

How did he get so cute?

How did she get so smart?

How did he get a lima bean stuck up his nose?

These are the day-to-day marvels that you can't always capture with a picture. They go unnoticed and years later, you're trying to remember exactly what your daughter's favorite song was, or the punchline to that silly joke that made your son laugh hysterically.

But you don't have time to write pages and pages about being a mom. You're too busy, you know, actually being one. You're kissing bruises, making lunches, and reading bedtime stories.

With *The Modern Mom's Memory Journal*, it's easy to keep track of all the ups and downs of motherhood—the good and the bad, the exhausting and the rewarding. Each day in this weekly journal is made up of fun and interesting prompts that you can fill out in a minute or two.

So turn the page and get started! By the time you finish the book, you'll have recorded a year's worth of wonderful memories that you can keep forever—all in less time than it takes to make your child's bowl of cereal each morning.

Monday

What was the cutest thing my child did today?

_____

_____

What did my kid smell like today? (Shampoo? Fruit punch? The family dog?)

_____

_____

What did I do today that I never would have done before I was a mom?

_____

_____

How much sleep did I get last night?

☐ **More than 8 hours:** I feel like a Disney princess!

☐ **Between 6 and 8 hours:** A few hits on the ol' snooze button, and I'm good to go.

☐ **Between 3 and 6 hours:** My face is permanently stuck in the yawn position.

☐ **Between 1 and 3 hours:** I now understand how zombies feel.

☐ **Sleep?** Hahaha! HAHAHAHA!

Extra Mom Notes:

_____

_____

_____

_____

_____

_____

Tuesday

The funniest thing my child did today was:

_____

_____

I ☐ did ☐ didn't laugh because:

_____

_____

What did I do today that made my child laugh?

_____

_____

If I could go back in time, what's one thing that I'd "do over" today?

_____

_____

Today I wished that I was my child's age so that I could

_____

_____ !

The mealtime breakdown:

___% Splattered against the wall   ___% Eaten by my kid

___% Hidden in the napkin   ___% Other: _____

___% Fed to the dog   _____

Extra Mom Notes:

_____

_____

_____

_____

_____

Wednesday

What's one thing my child did today that will embarrass him or her when he or she is a teenager?

_____
_____

Today's "Bad Mom" moment:

_____
_____

Today's "Best Mom Ever!" moment:

_____
_____

Based on my child's behavior today, I am sure he or she will grow up to be:

☐ A poet—so quiet and thoughtful!
☐ A boxer—so strong and tough!
☐ A political pundit—so loud and fussy!
☐ An Olympic sprinter—always on the go!
☐ A stand-up comedian—so funny and giggly!
☐ Other: _____ because _____

Extra Mom Notes:

_____
_____
_____
_____
_____
_____
_____
_____

Thursday

What's one lie I told my kid today? (That babies come from storks? That all of the nutrients are in the bread's crust?)

_____

_____

If a TV camera crew followed me around all day, they'd be filming:

☐ A wacky family sitcom, like *Everybody Loves Raymond* or *Modern Family*.

☐ A complex workplace drama, like *Grey's Anatomy* or *The Good Wife*.

☐ A cheesy soap opera, like *Days of Our Lives* or *General Hospital*.

☐ A hyperactive talent contest, like *America's Got Talent* or *So You Think You Can Dance*.

☐ Other: A _____ show, like

_____

The best actor to play my child would be _____,

because: _____

_____

Based on how I feel today, the best actress to play me would be

_____. She would be perfect because:

_____

_____

Extra Mom Notes:

_____

_____

_____

_____

_____

Friday Favorites! DATE

My child's favorite toy this week was _____

This week, my child's favorite friend was _____

If I had to describe this friend in one word, it would be _____
If I had to describe this friend's parents in one word, it would be
_____

The song my child listened to the most this week was
_____

My feelings about this song:
☐ Love it—one of my favorites!
☐ Like it.
☐ Tolerate it—it could be worse, I guess.
☐ Annoyed by it—it's starting to get on my nerves.
☐ Loathe it—it makes my ears bleed.

The food my child asked for the most this week was _____

I ☐ did ☐ didn't give him or her this food because:
_____
_____

My favorite mom activity is _____ because:
_____
_____

Extra Mom Notes:
_____
_____
_____
_____

Who was my parenting role model today? (Inspiration can come from anywhere, including your favorite TV character, your own parents, even the patient clerk at your local grocery store!)

_____

_____

If my child remembers one thing about today, I hope he or she remembers this:

_____

_____

Make Your Own Bedtime Story!

Once upon a time there was a _____ kid. That child had a mom who was really _____.

One day, the mom and the kid went on an adventure. First, they went to _____. There they met a big _____, who taught them both how to _____.

"_____!" said the kid. "This is the best _____ ever!"

Next, the mom and the kid went to _____. They played _____ and won!

"That was _____," said the mom, "but now let's go home."

So the mom and the kid went home and ate _____ for dinner. They brushed their teeth, put on their _____, and went to bed.

Extra Mom Notes:

_____

_____

_____

_____

_____

Sunday

Weekly Look Back

What's one thing that I learned about my child this week?

_____
_____
_____

What's one thing that my child learned about me this week?

_____
_____
_____

What's one thing that I learned about myself?

_____
_____
_____

What's my biggest hope for next week?

_____
_____
_____

Extra Mom Notes:

_____
_____
_____
_____
_____
_____
_____

Monday

What was the cutest thing my child did today?

_____

_____

What did my kid smell like today? (Shampoo? Fruit punch? The family dog?)

_____

_____

What did I do today that I never would have done before I was a mom?

_____

_____

How much sleep did I get last night?

☐ **More than 8 hours:** I feel like a Disney princess!

☐ **Between 6 and 8 hours:** A few hits on the ol' snooze button, and I'm good to go.

☐ **Between 3 and 6 hours:** My face is permanently stuck in the yawn position.

☐ **Between 1 and 3 hours:** I now understand how zombies feel.

☐ **Sleep?** Hahaha! HAHAHAHA!

Extra Mom Notes:

_____

_____

_____

_____

_____

_____

_____

Tuesday

The funniest thing my child did today was:

_____

_____

I ☐ did ☐ didn't laugh because:

_____

_____

What did I do today that made my child laugh?

_____

_____

If I could go back in time, what's one thing that I'd "do over" today?

_____

_____

Today I wished that I was my child's age so that I could

_____

_____!

The mealtime breakdown:

___% Splattered against the wall   ___% Eaten by my kid

___% Hidden in the napkin   ___% Other: _____

___% Fed to the dog   _____

Extra Mom Notes:

_____

_____

_____

_____

_____

Wednesday

What's one thing my child did today that will embarrass him or her when he or she is a teenager?

_____

_____

Today's "Bad Mom" moment:

_____

_____

Today's "Best Mom Ever!" moment:

_____

_____

Based on my child's behavior today, I am sure he or she will grow up to be:

☐ A poet—so quiet and thoughtful!

☐ A boxer—so strong and tough!

☐ A political pundit—so loud and fussy!

☐ An Olympic sprinter—always on the go!

☐ A stand-up comedian—so funny and giggly!

☐ Other: _____ because _____

Extra Mom Notes:

_____

_____

_____

_____

_____

_____

_____

_____

Thursday

What's one lie I told my kid today? (That babies come from storks?
That all of the nutrients are in the bread's crust?)

_____

_____

If a TV camera crew followed me around all day, they'd be filming:

☐ A wacky family sitcom, like _Everybody Loves Raymond_ or
   Modern Family.

☐ A complex workplace drama, like _Grey's Anatomy_ or _The Good Wife._

☐ A cheesy soap opera, like _Days of Our Lives_ or _General Hospital._

☐ A hyperactive talent contest, like _America's Got Talent_ or _So You
   Think You Can Dance._

☐ Other: A _____ show, like

_____

The best actor to play my child would be _____,
because: _____

_____

Based on how I feel today, the best actress to play me would be
_____. She would be perfect because:

_____

_____

Extra Mom Notes:

_____

_____

_____

_____

_____

Friday Favorites!

My child's favorite toy this week was _____

This week, my child's favorite friend was _____

If I had to describe this friend in one word, it would be _____
If I had to describe this friend's parents in one word, it would be
_____

The song my child listened to the most this week was
_____

My feelings about this song:
- ☐ Love it—one of my favorites!
- ☐ Like it.
- ☐ Tolerate it—it could be worse, I guess.
- ☐ Annoyed by it—it's starting to get on my nerves.
- ☐ Loathe it—it makes my ears bleed.

The food my child asked for the most this week was _____

I ☐ did ☐ didn't give him or her this food because:
_____
_____

My favorite mom activity is _____ because:
_____
_____

Extra Mom Notes:
_____
_____
_____
_____

Saturday

Who was my parenting role model today? (Inspiration can come from anywhere, including your favorite TV character, your own parents, even the patient clerk at your local grocery store!)

_____

_____

If my child remembers one thing about today, I hope he or she remembers this:

_____

_____

Make Your Own Bedtime Story!

Once upon a time there was a _____ kid. That child had a mom who was really _____.

One day, the mom and the kid went on an adventure. First, they went to _____. There they met a big _____, who taught them both how to _____.

"_____!" said the kid. "This is the best _____ ever!"

Next, the mom and the kid went to _____. They played _____ and won!

"That was _____," said the mom, "but now let's go home."

So the mom and the kid went home and ate _____ for dinner.

They brushed their teeth, put on their _____, and went to bed.

Extra Mom Notes:

_____

_____

_____

_____

_____

Sunday

Weekly Look Back

What's one thing that I learned about my child this week?

_____

_____

_____

What's one thing that my child learned about me this week?

_____

_____

_____

What's one thing that I learned about myself?

_____

_____

_____

What's my biggest hope for next week?

_____

_____

_____

Extra Mom Notes:

_____

_____

_____

_____

_____

_____

_____

Monday

What was the cutest thing my child did today?

_____

_____

What did my kid smell like today? (Shampoo? Fruit punch? The family dog?)

_____

_____

What did I do today that I never would have done before I was a mom?

_____

_____

How much sleep did I get last night?

☐ More than 8 hours: I feel like a Disney princess!

☐ Between 6 and 8 hours: A few hits on the ol' snooze button, and I'm good to go.

☐ Between 3 and 6 hours: My face is permanently stuck in the yawn position.

☐ Between 1 and 3 hours: I now understand how zombies feel.

☐ Sleep? Hahaha! HAHAHAHA!

Extra Mom Notes:

_____

_____

_____

_____

_____

_____

The funniest thing my child did today was:

_____

_____

I ☐ did ☐ didn't laugh because:

_____

_____

What did I do today that made my child laugh?

_____

_____

If I could go back in time, what's one thing that I'd "do over" today?

_____

_____

Today I wished that I was my child's age so that I could

_____

_____!

The mealtime breakdown:

____% Splattered against the wall   ____% Eaten by my kid

____% Hidden in the napkin   ____% Other: _____

____% Fed to the dog   _____

Extra Mom Notes:

_____

_____

_____

_____

_____

_____

Wednesday

What's one thing my child did today that will embarrass him or her when he or she is a teenager?

_____

_____

Today's "Bad Mom" moment:

_____

_____

Today's "Best Mom Ever!" moment:

_____

_____

Based on my child's behavior today, I am sure he or she will grow up to be:

☐ A poet—so quiet and thoughtful!

☐ A boxer—so strong and tough!

☐ A political pundit—so loud and fussy!

☐ An Olympic sprinter—always on the go!

☐ A stand-up comedian—so funny and giggly!

☐ Other: _____ because _____

Extra Mom Notes:

_____

_____

_____

_____

_____

_____

_____

_____

Thursday

What's one lie I told my kid today? (That babies come from storks? That all of the nutrients are in the bread's crust?)

_____

_____

If a TV camera crew followed me around all day, they'd be filming:

☐ A wacky family sitcom, like *Everybody Loves Raymond* or *Modern Family.*

☐ A complex workplace drama, like *Grey's Anatomy* or *The Good Wife.*

☐ A cheesy soap opera, like *Days of Our Lives* or *General Hospital.*

☐ A hyperactive talent contest, like *America's Got Talent* or *So You Think You Can Dance.*

☐ Other: A _____ show, like

_____

The best actor to play my child would be _____,
because: _____

_____

Based on how I feel today, the best actress to play me would be

_____. She would be perfect because:

_____

_____

Extra Mom Notes:

_____

_____

_____

_____

_____

Friday Favorites! DATE

My child's favorite toy this week was _____

This week, my child's favorite friend was _____

If I had to describe this friend in one word, it would be _____
If I had to describe this friend's parents in one word, it would be
_____

The song my child listened to the most this week was
_____

My feelings about this song:
☐ Love it—one of my favorites!
☐ Like it.
☐ Tolerate it—it could be worse, I guess.
☐ Annoyed by it—it's starting to get on my nerves.
☐ Loathe it—it makes my ears bleed.

The food my child asked for the most this week was _____

I ☐ did ☐ didn't give him or her this food because:
_____
_____

My favorite mom activity is _____ because:
_____
_____

Extra Mom Notes:
_____
_____
_____
_____

Saturday

Who was my parenting role model today? (Inspiration can come from anywhere, including your favorite TV character, your own parents, even the patient clerk at your local grocery store!)

_____

_____

If my child remembers one thing about today, I hope he or she remembers this:

_____

_____

Make Your Own Bedtime Story!

Once upon a time there was a _____ kid. That child had a mom who was really _____.

One day, the mom and the kid went on an adventure. First, they went to _____. There they met a big _____, who taught them both how to _____.

"_____!" said the kid. "This is the best _____ ever!"

Next, the mom and the kid went to _____. They played _____ and won!

"That was _____," said the mom, "but now let's go home."

So the mom and the kid went home and ate _____ for dinner. They brushed their teeth, put on their _____, and went to bed.

Extra Mom Notes:

_____

_____

_____

_____

_____

Sunday

Weekly Look Back

What's one thing that I learned about my child this week?

_____
_____
_____

What's one thing that my child learned about me this week?

_____
_____
_____

What's one thing that I learned about myself?

_____
_____
_____

What's my biggest hope for next week?

_____
_____
_____

Extra Mom Notes:

_____
_____
_____
_____
_____
_____
_____
_____

Monday

What was the cutest thing my child did today?

_____

_____

What did my kid smell like today? (Shampoo? Fruit punch? The family dog?)

_____

_____

What did I do today that I never would have done before I was a mom?

_____

_____

How much sleep did I get last night?

☐ More than 8 hours: I feel like a Disney princess!

☐ Between 6 and 8 hours: A few hits on the ol' snooze button, and I'm good to go.

☐ Between 3 and 6 hours: My face is permanently stuck in the yawn position.

☐ Between 1 and 3 hours: I now understand how zombies feel.

☐ Sleep? Hahaha! HAHAHAHA!

Extra Mom Notes:

_____

_____

_____

_____

_____

_____

Tuesday

DATE

The funniest thing my child did today was:

_____

_____

I ☐ did ☐ didn't laugh because:

_____

_____

What did I do today that made my child laugh?

_____

_____

If I could go back in time, what's one thing that I'd "do over" today?

_____

_____

Today I wished that I was my child's age so that I could

_____

_____!

The mealtime breakdown:

____% Splattered against the wall   ____% Eaten by my kid

____% Hidden in the napkin   ____% Other: _____

____% Fed to the dog   _____

Extra Mom Notes:

_____

_____

_____

_____

_____

_____

Wednesday

What's one thing my child did today that will embarrass him or her when he or she is a teenager?

_____

_____

Today's "Bad Mom" moment:

_____

_____

Today's "Best Mom Ever!" moment:

_____

_____

Based on my child's behavior today, I am sure he or she will grow up to be:

☐ A poet—so quiet and thoughtful!

☐ A boxer—so strong and tough!

☐ A political pundit—so loud and fussy!

☐ An Olympic sprinter—always on the go!

☐ A stand-up comedian—so funny and giggly!

☐ Other: _____ because _____

Extra Mom Notes:

_____

_____

_____

_____

_____

_____

_____

_____

Thursday

What's one lie I told my kid today? (That babies come from storks? That all of the nutrients are in the bread's crust?)

_____

_____

If a TV camera crew followed me around all day, they'd be filming:

☐ A wacky family sitcom, like _Everybody Loves Raymond_ or _Modern Family._

☐ A complex workplace drama, like _Grey's Anatomy_ or _The Good Wife._

☐ A cheesy soap opera, like _Days of Our Lives_ or _General Hospital._

☐ A hyperactive talent contest, like _America's Got Talent_ or _So You Think You Can Dance._

☐ Other: A _____ show, like

_____

The best actor to play my child would be _____,

because: _____

_____

Based on how I feel today, the best actress to play me would be

_____. She would be perfect because:

_____

_____

Extra Mom Notes:

_____

_____

_____

_____

_____

Friday Favorites!

My child's favorite toy this week was _____

This week, my child's favorite friend was _____

If I had to describe this friend in one word, it would be _____
If I had to describe this friend's parents in one word, it would be

_____

The song my child listened to the most this week was

_____

My feelings about this song:
☐ Love it—one of my favorites!
☐ Like it.
☐ Tolerate it—it could be worse, I guess.
☐ Annoyed by it—it's starting to get on my nerves.
☐ Loathe it—it makes my ears bleed.

The food my child asked for the most this week was _____

I ☐ did ☐ didn't give him or her this food because:

_____

_____

My favorite mom activity is _____ because:

_____

_____

Extra Mom Notes:

_____

_____

_____

_____

Saturday

Who was my parenting role model today? (Inspiration can come from anywhere, including your favorite TV character, your own parents, even the patient clerk at your local grocery store!)

_____

_____

If my child remembers one thing about today, I hope he or she remembers this:

_____

_____

Make Your Own Bedtime Story!

Once upon a time there was a _____ kid. That child had a mom who was really _____.

One day, the mom and the kid went on an adventure. First, they went to _____. There they met a big _____, who taught them both how to _____.

"_____!" said the kid. "This is the best _____ ever!"

Next, the mom and the kid went to _____. They played _____ and won!

"That was _____," said the mom, "but now let's go home."

So the mom and the kid went home and ate _____ for dinner. They brushed their teeth, put on their _____, and went to bed.

Extra Mom Notes:

_____

_____

_____

_____

_____

Sunday

Weekly Look Back

What's one thing that I learned about my child this week?

_____
_____
_____

What's one thing that my child learned about me this week?

_____
_____
_____

What's one thing that I learned about myself?

_____
_____
_____

What's my biggest hope for next week?

_____
_____
_____

Extra Mom Notes:

_____
_____
_____
_____
_____
_____
_____

Monday

What was the cutest thing my child did today?

_____

_____

**What did my kid smell like today? (Shampoo? Fruit punch?
The family dog?)**

_____

_____

**What did I do today that I never would have done before I was
a mom?**

_____

_____

How much sleep did I get last night?

☐ **More than 8 hours:** I feel like a Disney princess!

☐ **Between 6 and 8 hours:** A few hits on the ol' snooze button, and
I'm good to go.

☐ **Between 3 and 6 hours:** My face is permanently stuck in the yawn
position.

☐ **Between 1 and 3 hours:** I now understand how zombies feel.

☐ **Sleep?** Hahaha! HAHAHAHA!

Extra Mom Notes:

_____

_____

_____

_____

_____

_____

_____

DATE _____

Tuesday

The funniest thing my child did today was:

_____

_____

I ☐ did ☐ didn't laugh because:

_____

_____

What did I do today that made my child laugh?

_____

_____

If I could go back in time, what's one thing that I'd "do over" today?

_____

_____

Today I wished that I was my child's age so that I could

_____

_____ !

The mealtime breakdown:

____% Splattered against the wall   ____% Eaten by my kid

____% Hidden in the napkin   ____% Other: _____

____% Fed to the dog   _____

Extra Mom Notes:

_____

_____

_____

_____

_____

_____

Wednesday

What's one thing my child did today that will embarrass him or her when he or she is a teenager?

_____

_____

Today's "Bad Mom" moment:

_____

_____

Today's "Best Mom Ever!" moment:

_____

_____

Based on my child's behavior today, I am sure he or she will grow up to be:

☐ A poet—so quiet and thoughtful!

☐ A boxer—so strong and tough!

☐ A political pundit—so loud and fussy!

☐ An Olympic sprinter—always on the go!

☐ A stand-up comedian—so funny and giggly!

☐ Other: _____ because _____

Extra Mom Notes:

_____

_____

_____

_____

_____

_____

_____

_____

Thursday

What's one lie I told my kid today? (That babies come from storks? That all of the nutrients are in the bread's crust?)

_____

_____

If a TV camera crew followed me around all day, they'd be filming:

☐ A wacky family sitcom, like *Everybody Loves Raymond* or *Modern Family*.

☐ A complex workplace drama, like *Grey's Anatomy* or *The Good Wife*.

☐ A cheesy soap opera, like *Days of Our Lives* or *General Hospital*.

☐ A hyperactive talent contest, like *America's Got Talent* or *So You Think You Can Dance*.

☐ Other: A _____ show, like

_____

The best actor to play my child would be _____,
because: _____

_____

Based on how I feel today, the best actress to play me would be
_____. She would be perfect because:

_____

_____

Extra Mom Notes:

_____

_____

_____

_____

_____

Friday Favorites! DATE _____

My child's favorite toy this week was _____

This week, my child's favorite friend was _____

If I had to describe this friend in one word, it would be _____
If I had to describe this friend's parents in one word, it would be
_____

The song my child listened to the most this week was
_____

My feelings about this song:
☐ Love it—one of my favorites!
☐ Like it.
☐ Tolerate it—it could be worse, I guess.
☐ Annoyed by it—it's starting to get on my nerves.
☐ Loathe it—it makes my ears bleed.

The food my child asked for the most this week was _____

I ☐ did ☐ didn't give him or her this food because:
_____
_____

My favorite mom activity is _____ because:
_____
_____

Extra Mom Notes:
_____
_____
_____
_____

Saturday

Who was my parenting role model today? (Inspiration can come from anywhere, including your favorite TV character, your own parents, even the patient clerk at your local grocery store!)

_____

_____

If my child remembers one thing about today, I hope he or she remembers this:

_____

_____

Make Your Own Bedtime Story!

Once upon a time there was a _____ kid. That child had a mom who was really _____.

One day, the mom and the kid went on an adventure. First, they went to _____. There they met a big _____, who taught them both how to _____.

"_____!" said the kid. "This is the best _____ ever!"

Next, the mom and the kid went to _____. They played _____ and won!

"That was _____," said the mom, "but now let's go home."

So the mom and the kid went home and ate _____ for dinner. They brushed their teeth, put on their _____, and went to bed.

Extra Mom Notes:

_____

_____

_____

_____

_____

Sunday

Weekly Look Back

What's one thing that I learned about my child this week?

_____
_____
_____

What's one thing that my child learned about me this week?

_____
_____
_____

What's one thing that I learned about myself?

_____
_____
_____

What's my biggest hope for next week?

_____
_____
_____

Extra Mom Notes:

_____
_____
_____
_____
_____
_____
_____

Monday

What was the cutest thing my child did today?

_____

_____

What did my kid smell like today? (Shampoo? Fruit punch? The family dog?)

_____

_____

What did I do today that I never would have done before I was a mom?

_____

_____

How much sleep did I get last night?

☐ **More than 8 hours:** I feel like a Disney princess!

☐ **Between 6 and 8 hours:** A few hits on the ol' snooze button, and I'm good to go.

☐ **Between 3 and 6 hours:** My face is permanently stuck in the yawn position.

☐ **Between 1 and 3 hours:** I now understand how zombies feel.

☐ **Sleep?** Hahaha! HAHAHAHA!

Extra Mom Notes:

_____

_____

_____

_____

_____

_____

Tuesday

The funniest thing my child did today was:

_____

_____

I ☐ did ☐ didn't laugh because:

_____

_____

What did I do today that made my child laugh?

_____

_____

If I could go back in time, what's one thing that I'd "do over" today?

_____

_____

Today I wished that I was my child's age so that I could

_____

_____!

The mealtime breakdown:

___% Splattered against the wall   ___% Eaten by my kid

___% Hidden in the napkin   ___% Other: _____

___% Fed to the dog   _____

Extra Mom Notes:

_____

_____

_____

_____

_____

Wednesday

What's one thing my child did today that will embarrass him or her when he or she is a teenager?

_____

_____

Today's "Bad Mom" moment:

_____

_____

Today's "Best Mom Ever!" moment:

_____

_____

Based on my child's behavior today, I am sure he or she will grow up to be:

☐ A poet—so quiet and thoughtful!

☐ A boxer—so strong and tough!

☐ A political pundit—so loud and fussy!

☐ An Olympic sprinter—always on the go!

☐ A stand-up comedian—so funny and giggly!

☐ Other: _____ because _____

Extra Mom Notes:

_____

_____

_____

_____

_____

_____

_____

_____

Thursday

What's one lie I told my kid today? (That babies come from storks?
That all of the nutrients are in the bread's crust?)

_____

_____

If a TV camera crew followed me around all day, they'd be filming:

☐ A wacky family sitcom, like _Everybody Loves Raymond_ or
  Modern Family.

☐ A complex workplace drama, like _Grey's Anatomy_ or _The Good Wife._

☐ A cheesy soap opera, like _Days of Our Lives_ or _General Hospital._

☐ A hyperactive talent contest, like _America's Got Talent_ or _So You
  Think You Can Dance._

☐ Other: A _____ show, like
  _____

The best actor to play my child would be _____,

because: _____

_____

Based on how I feel today, the best actress to play me would be
_____. She would be perfect because:

_____

_____

Extra Mom Notes:

_____

_____

_____

_____

_____

Friday Favorites!

My child's favorite toy this week was _____

This week, my child's favorite friend was _____

If I had to describe this friend in one word, it would be _____
If I had to describe this friend's parents in one word, it would be

_____

The song my child listened to the most this week was

_____

My feelings about this song:
☐ Love it—one of my favorites!
☐ Like it.
☐ Tolerate it—it could be worse, I guess.
☐ Annoyed by it—it's starting to get on my nerves.
☐ Loathe it—it makes my ears bleed.

The food my child asked for the most this week was _____

I ☐ did ☐ didn't give him or her this food because:
_____
_____

My favorite mom activity is _____ because:
_____
_____

Extra Mom Notes:
_____
_____
_____
_____

Saturday

Who was my parenting role model today? (Inspiration can come from anywhere, including your favorite TV character, your own parents, even the patient clerk at your local grocery store!)

_____

_____

If my child remembers one thing about today, I hope he or she remembers this:

_____

_____

Make Your Own Bedtime Story!

Once upon a time there was a _____ kid. That child had a mom who was really _____.

One day, the mom and the kid went on an adventure. First, they went to _____. There they met a big _____, who taught them both how to _____.

"_____!" said the kid. "This is the best _____ ever!"

Next, the mom and the kid went to _____. They played _____ and won!

"That was _____," said the mom, "but now let's go home."

So the mom and the kid went home and ate _____ for dinner. They brushed their teeth, put on their _____, and went to bed.

Extra Mom Notes:

_____

_____

_____

_____

_____

Sunday

Weekly Look Back

What's one thing that I learned about my child this week?

_____
_____
_____

What's one thing that my child learned about me this week?

_____
_____
_____

What's one thing that I learned about myself?

_____
_____
_____

What's my biggest hope for next week?

_____
_____
_____

Extra Mom Notes:

_____
_____
_____
_____
_____
_____
_____

Monday

What was the cutest thing my child did today?

_____

_____

What did my kid smell like today? (Shampoo? Fruit punch? The family dog?)

_____

_____

What did I do today that I never would have done before I was a mom?

_____

_____

How much sleep did I get last night?

☐ **More than 8 hours:** I feel like a Disney princess!

☐ **Between 6 and 8 hours:** A few hits on the ol' snooze button, and I'm good to go.

☐ **Between 3 and 6 hours:** My face is permanently stuck in the yawn position.

☐ **Between 1 and 3 hours:** I now understand how zombies feel.

☐ **Sleep?** Hahaha! HAHAHAHA!

Extra Mom Notes:

_____

_____

_____

_____

_____

_____

_____

Tuesday

The funniest thing my child did today was:

_____

_____

I ☐ did ☐ didn't laugh because:

_____

_____

What did I do today that made my child laugh?

_____

_____

If I could go back in time, what's one thing that I'd "do over" today?

_____

_____

Today I wished that I was my child's age so that I could

_____

_____ !

The mealtime breakdown:

___% Splattered against the wall   ___% Eaten by my kid

___% Hidden in the napkin   ___% Other: _____

___% Fed to the dog   _____

Extra Mom Notes:

_____

_____

_____

_____

_____

Wednesday

What's one thing my child did today that will embarrass him or her when he or she is a teenager?

_____

_____

Today's "Bad Mom" moment:

_____

_____

Today's "Best Mom Ever!" moment:

_____

_____

Based on my child's behavior today, I am sure he or she will grow up to be:

☐ A poet—so quiet and thoughtful!

☐ A boxer—so strong and tough!

☐ A political pundit—so loud and fussy!

☐ An Olympic sprinter—always on the go!

☐ A stand-up comedian—so funny and giggly!

☐ Other: _____ because _____

Extra Mom Notes:

_____

_____

_____

_____

_____

_____

_____

_____

Thursday

What's one lie I told my kid today? (That babies come from storks? That all of the nutrients are in the bread's crust?)

_____

_____

If a TV camera crew followed me around all day, they'd be filming:

☐ A wacky family sitcom, like _Everybody Loves Raymond_ or _Modern Family_.

☐ A complex workplace drama, like _Grey's Anatomy_ or _The Good Wife_.

☐ A cheesy soap opera, like _Days of Our Lives_ or _General Hospital_.

☐ A hyperactive talent contest, like _America's Got Talent_ or _So You Think You Can Dance_.

☐ Other: A _____ show, like

_____

The best actor to play my child would be _____,

because: _____

_____

Based on how I feel today, the best actress to play me would be

_____. She would be perfect because:

_____

_____

Extra Mom Notes:

_____

_____

_____

_____

_____

Friday Favorites! DATE _____

My child's favorite toy this week was _____

This week, my child's favorite friend was _____

If I had to describe this friend in one word, it would be _____
If I had to describe this friend's parents in one word, it would be
_____

The song my child listened to the most this week was
_____

My feelings about this song:
- ☐ Love it—one of my favorites!
- ☐ Like it.
- ☐ Tolerate it—it could be worse, I guess.
- ☐ Annoyed by it—it's starting to get on my nerves.
- ☐ Loathe it—it makes my ears bleed.

The food my child asked for the most this week was _____

I ☐ did ☐ didn't give him or her this food because:
_____
_____

My favorite mom activity is _____ because:
_____
_____

Extra Mom Notes:
_____
_____
_____
_____

Who was my parenting role model today? (Inspiration can come from anywhere, including your favorite TV character, your own parents, even the patient clerk at your local grocery store!)

_____

_____

If my child remembers one thing about today, I hope he or she remembers this:

_____

_____

Make Your Own Bedtime Story!

Once upon a time there was a _____ kid. That child had a mom who was really _____.

One day, the mom and the kid went on an adventure. First, they went to _____. There they met a big _____, who taught them both how to _____.

"_____!" said the kid. "This is the best _____ ever!"

Next, the mom and the kid went to _____. They played _____ and won!

"That was _____," said the mom, "but now let's go home."

So the mom and the kid went home and ate _____ for dinner. They brushed their teeth, put on their _____, and went to bed.

Extra Mom Notes:

_____

_____

_____

_____

_____

Sunday

DATE

Weekly Look Back

What's one thing that I learned about my child this week?

_____
_____
_____

What's one thing that my child learned about me this week?

_____
_____
_____

What's one thing that I learned about myself?

_____
_____
_____

What's my biggest hope for next week?

_____
_____
_____

Extra Mom Notes:

_____
_____
_____
_____
_____
_____

Monday

What was the cutest thing my child did today?

_____

_____

What did my kid smell like today? (Shampoo? Fruit punch? The family dog?)

_____

_____

What did I do today that I never would have done before I was a mom?

_____

_____

How much sleep did I get last night?

☐ More than 8 hours: I feel like a Disney princess!

☐ Between 6 and 8 hours: A few hits on the ol' snooze button, and I'm good to go.

☐ Between 3 and 6 hours: My face is permanently stuck in the yawn position.

☐ Between 1 and 3 hours: I now understand how zombies feel.

☐ Sleep? Hahaha! HAHAHAHA!

Extra Mom Notes:

_____

_____

_____

_____

_____

_____

Tuesday

DATE

The funniest thing my child did today was:

_____

_____

I ☐ did ☐ didn't laugh because:

_____

_____

What did I do today that made my child laugh?

_____

_____

If I could go back in time, what's one thing that I'd "do over" today?

_____

_____

Today I wished that I was my child's age so that I could

_____

_____!

The mealtime breakdown:

___% Splattered against the wall   ___% Eaten by my kid

___% Hidden in the napkin   ___% Other: _____

___% Fed to the dog

Extra Mom Notes:

_____

_____

_____

_____

_____

_____

Wednesday

What's one thing my child did today that will embarrass him or her when he or she is a teenager?

_____

_____

Today's "Bad Mom" moment:

_____

_____

Today's "Best Mom Ever!" moment:

_____

_____

Based on my child's behavior today, I am sure he or she will grow up to be:

☐ A poet—so quiet and thoughtful!

☐ A boxer—so strong and tough!

☐ A political pundit—so loud and fussy!

☐ An Olympic sprinter—always on the go!

☐ A stand-up comedian—so funny and giggly!

☐ Other: _____ because _____

Extra Mom Notes:

_____

_____

_____

_____

_____

_____

_____

_____

Thursday

What's one lie I told my kid today? (That babies come from storks? That all of the nutrients are in the bread's crust?)

_____

_____

If a TV camera crew followed me around all day, they'd be filming:

☐ A wacky family sitcom, like _Everybody Loves Raymond_ or _Modern Family_.

☐ A complex workplace drama, like _Grey's Anatomy_ or _The Good Wife_.

☐ A cheesy soap opera, like _Days of Our Lives_ or _General Hospital_.

☐ A hyperactive talent contest, like _America's Got Talent_ or _So You Think You Can Dance_.

☐ Other: A _____ show, like

_____

The best actor to play my child would be _____,

because: _____

_____

Based on how I feel today, the best actress to play me would be

_____. She would be perfect because:

_____

_____

Extra Mom Notes:

_____

_____

_____

_____

Friday Favorites!

My child's favorite toy this week was _____

This week, my child's favorite friend was _____

If I had to describe this friend in one word, it would be _____
If I had to describe this friend's parents in one word, it would be
_____

The song my child listened to the most this week was
_____

My feelings about this song:
- ☐ Love it—one of my favorites!
- ☐ Like it.
- ☐ Tolerate it—it could be worse, I guess.
- ☐ Annoyed by it—it's starting to get on my nerves.
- ☐ Loathe it—it makes my ears bleed.

The food my child asked for the most this week was _____

I ☐ did ☐ didn't give him or her this food because:
_____
_____

My favorite mom activity is _____ because:
_____
_____

Extra Mom Notes:
_____
_____
_____
_____

Saturday

Who was my parenting role model today? (Inspiration can come from anywhere, including your favorite TV character, your own parents, even the patient clerk at your local grocery store!)

_____

_____

If my child remembers one thing about today, I hope he or she remembers this:

_____

_____

Make Your Own Bedtime Story!

Once upon a time there was a _____ kid. That child had a mom who was really _____.

One day, the mom and the kid went on an adventure. First, they went to _____. There they met a big _____, who taught them both how to _____.

"_____!" said the kid. "This is the best _____ ever!"

Next, the mom and the kid went to _____. They played _____ and won!

"That was _____," said the mom, "but now let's go home."

So the mom and the kid went home and ate _____ for dinner. They brushed their teeth, put on their _____, and went to bed.

Extra Mom Notes:

_____

_____

_____

_____

_____

Weekly Look Back

What's one thing that I learned about my child this week?

_____
_____
_____

What's one thing that my child learned about me this week?

_____
_____
_____

What's one thing that I learned about myself?

_____
_____
_____

What's my biggest hope for next week?

_____
_____
_____

Extra Mom Notes:

_____
_____
_____
_____
_____
_____
_____

Monday

What was the cutest thing my child did today?

_____

_____

What did my kid smell like today? (Shampoo? Fruit punch? The family dog?)

_____

_____

What did I do today that I never would have done before I was a mom?

_____

_____

How much sleep did I get last night?

☐ **More than 8 hours:** I feel like a Disney princess!

☐ **Between 6 and 8 hours:** A few hits on the ol' snooze button, and I'm good to go.

☐ **Between 3 and 6 hours:** My face is permanently stuck in the yawn position.

☐ **Between 1 and 3 hours:** I now understand how zombies feel.

☐ **Sleep?** Hahaha! HAHAHAHA!

Extra Mom Notes:

_____

_____

_____

_____

_____

_____

DATE

Tuesday

The funniest thing my child did today was:

_____

_____

I ☐ did ☐ didn't laugh because:

_____

_____

What did I do today that made my child laugh?

_____

_____

If I could go back in time, what's one thing that I'd "do over" today?

_____

_____

Today I wished that I was my child's age so that I could

_____

_____!

The mealtime breakdown:

___% Splattered against the wall   ___% Eaten by my kid

___% Hidden in the napkin   ___% Other: _____

___% Fed to the dog   _____

Extra Mom Notes:

_____

_____

_____

_____

_____

_____

Wednesday

What's one thing my child did today that will embarrass him or her when he or she is a teenager?

_____

_____

Today's "Bad Mom" moment:

_____

_____

Today's "Best Mom Ever!" moment:

_____

_____

Based on my child's behavior today, I am sure he or she will grow up to be:

☐ A poet—so quiet and thoughtful!

☐ A boxer—so strong and tough!

☐ A political pundit—so loud and fussy!

☐ An Olympic sprinter—always on the go!

☐ A stand-up comedian—so funny and giggly!

☐ Other: _____ because _____

Extra Mom Notes:

_____

_____

_____

_____

_____

_____

_____

_____

Thursday

What's one lie I told my kid today? (That babies come from storks? That all of the nutrients are in the bread's crust?)

_____

_____

If a TV camera crew followed me around all day, they'd be filming:

☐ A wacky family sitcom, like _Everybody Loves Raymond_ or _Modern Family._

☐ A complex workplace drama, like _Grey's Anatomy_ or _The Good Wife._

☐ A cheesy soap opera, like _Days of Our Lives_ or _General Hospital._

☐ A hyperactive talent contest, like _America's Got Talent_ or _So You Think You Can Dance._

☐ Other: A _____ show, like

_____

The best actor to play my child would be _____,
because: _____

_____

Based on how I feel today, the best actress to play me would be

_____. She would be perfect because:

_____

_____

Extra Mom Notes:

_____

_____

_____

_____

_____

Friday Favorites! DATE

My child's favorite toy this week was _____

This week, my child's favorite friend was _____

If I had to describe this friend in one word, it would be _____
If I had to describe this friend's parents in one word, it would be
_____

The song my child listened to the most this week was
_____

My feelings about this song:
- ☐ Love it—one of my favorites!
- ☐ Like it.
- ☐ Tolerate it—it could be worse, I guess.
- ☐ Annoyed by it—it's starting to get on my nerves.
- ☐ Loathe it—it makes my ears bleed.

The food my child asked for the most this week was _____

I ☐ did ☐ didn't give him or her this food because:
_____
_____

My favorite mom activity is _____ because:
_____
_____

Extra Mom Notes:
_____
_____
_____
_____

Who was my parenting role model today? (Inspiration can come from anywhere, including your favorite TV character, your own parents, even the patient clerk at your local grocery store!)

_____

_____

If my child remembers one thing about today, I hope he or she remembers this:

_____

_____

Make Your Own Bedtime Story!

Once upon a time there was a _____ kid. That child had a mom who was really _____.

One day, the mom and the kid went on an adventure. First, they went to _____. There they met a big _____, who taught them both how to _____.

"_____!" said the kid. "This is the best _____ ever!"

Next, the mom and the kid went to _____. They played _____ and won!

"That was _____," said the mom, "but now let's go home."

So the mom and the kid went home and ate _____ for dinner. They brushed their teeth, put on their _____, and went to bed.

Extra Mom Notes:

_____

_____

_____

_____

_____

Sunday

Weekly Look Back

What's one thing that I learned about my child this week?

_____

_____

_____

What's one thing that my child learned about me this week?

_____

_____

_____

What's one thing that I learned about myself?

_____

_____

_____

What's my biggest hope for next week?

_____

_____

_____

Extra Mom Notes:

_____

_____

_____

_____

_____

_____

_____

What was the cutest thing my child did today?

_____

_____

What did my kid smell like today? (Shampoo? Fruit punch? The family dog?)

_____

_____

What did I do today that I never would have done before I was a mom?

_____

_____

How much sleep did I get last night?

☐ **More than 8 hours:** I feel like a Disney princess!

☐ **Between 6 and 8 hours:** A few hits on the ol' snooze button, and I'm good to go.

☐ **Between 3 and 6 hours:** My face is permanently stuck in the yawn position.

☐ **Between 1 and 3 hours:** I now understand how zombies feel.

☐ **Sleep?** Hahaha! HAHAHAHA!

Extra Mom Notes:

_____

_____

_____

_____

_____

_____

_____

Tuesday

DATE

The funniest thing my child did today was:

_____

_____

I ☐ did ☐ didn't laugh because:

_____

_____

What did I do today that made my child laugh?

_____

_____

If I could go back in time, what's one thing that I'd "do over" today?

_____

_____

Today I wished that I was my child's age so that I could

_____

_____!

The mealtime breakdown:

___% Splattered against the wall   ___% Eaten by my kid

___% Hidden in the napkin   ___% Other: _____

___% Fed to the dog   _____

Extra Mom Notes:

_____

_____

_____

_____

_____

_____

What's one thing my child did today that will embarrass him or her when he or she is a teenager?

_____

_____

Today's "Bad Mom" moment:

_____

_____

Today's "Best Mom Ever!" moment:

_____

_____

Based on my child's behavior today, I am sure he or she will grow up to be:

☐ A poet—so quiet and thoughtful!

☐ A boxer—so strong and tough!

☐ A political pundit—so loud and fussy!

☐ An Olympic sprinter—always on the go!

☐ A stand-up comedian—so funny and giggly!

☐ Other: _____ because _____

Extra Mom Notes:

_____

_____

_____

_____

_____

_____

_____

_____

Thursday

What's one lie I told my kid today? (That babies come from storks? That all of the nutrients are in the bread's crust?)

_____

_____

If a TV camera crew followed me around all day, they'd be filming:

☐ A wacky family sitcom, like _Everybody Loves Raymond_ or _Modern Family._

☐ A complex workplace drama, like _Grey's Anatomy_ or _The Good Wife._

☐ A cheesy soap opera, like _Days of Our Lives_ or _General Hospital._

☐ A hyperactive talent contest, like _America's Got Talent_ or _So You Think You Can Dance._

☐ Other: A _____ show, like

_____

The best actor to play my child would be _____,
because: _____

_____

Based on how I feel today, the best actress to play me would be
_____. She would be perfect because:

_____

_____

Extra Mom Notes:

_____

_____

_____

_____

_____

Friday Favorites!

My child's favorite toy this week was _____

This week, my child's favorite friend was _____

If I had to describe this friend in one word, it would be _____
If I had to describe this friend's parents in one word, it would be
_____

The song my child listened to the most this week was
_____

My feelings about this song:
☐ Love it—one of my favorites!
☐ Like it.
☐ Tolerate it—it could be worse, I guess.
☐ Annoyed by it—it's starting to get on my nerves.
☐ Loathe it—it makes my ears bleed.

The food my child asked for the most this week was _____

I ☐ did ☐ didn't   give him or her this food because:
_____
_____

My favorite mom activity is _____ because:
_____
_____

Extra Mom Notes:
_____
_____
_____
_____

Saturday

Who was my parenting role model today? (Inspiration can come from anywhere, including your favorite TV character, your own parents, even the patient clerk at your local grocery store!)

_____

_____

If my child remembers one thing about today, I hope he or she remembers this:

_____

_____

Make Your Own Bedtime Story!

Once upon a time there was a _____ kid. That child had a mom who was really _____.

One day, the mom and the kid went on an adventure. First, they went to _____. There they met a big _____, who taught them both how to _____.

"_____!" said the kid. "This is the best _____ ever!"

Next, the mom and the kid went to _____. They played _____ and won!

"That was _____," said the mom, "but now let's go home."

So the mom and the kid went home and ate _____ for dinner.

They brushed their teeth, put on their _____, and went to bed.

Extra Mom Notes:

_____

_____

_____

_____

_____

Weekly Look Back

What's one thing that I learned about my child this week?

_____
_____
_____

What's one thing that my child learned about me this week?

_____
_____
_____

What's one thing that I learned about myself?

_____
_____
_____

What's my biggest hope for next week?

_____
_____
_____

Extra Mom Notes:

_____
_____
_____
_____
_____
_____
_____
_____

Monday

What was the cutest thing my child did today?

_____

_____

What did my kid smell like today? (Shampoo? Fruit punch? The family dog?)

_____

_____

What did I do today that I never would have done before I was a mom?

_____

_____

How much sleep did I get last night?

☐ More than 8 hours: I feel like a Disney princess!

☐ Between 6 and 8 hours: A few hits on the ol' snooze button, and I'm good to go.

☐ Between 3 and 6 hours: My face is permanently stuck in the yawn position.

☐ Between 1 and 3 hours: I now understand how zombies feel.

☐ Sleep? Hahaha! HAHAHAHA!

Extra Mom Notes:

_____

_____

_____

_____

_____

_____

_____

Tuesday

The funniest thing my child did today was:

_____

_____

I ☐ **did** ☐ **didn't laugh because:**

_____

_____

What did I do today that made my child laugh?

_____

_____

If I could go back in time, what's one thing that I'd "do over" today?

_____

_____

Today I wished that I was my child's age so that I could

_____

_____ !

The mealtime breakdown:

___% Splattered against the wall   ___% Eaten by my kid

___% Hidden in the napkin   ___% Other: _____

___% Fed to the dog   _____

Extra Mom Notes:

_____

_____

_____

_____

_____

_____

Wednesday

What's one thing my child did today that will embarrass him or her when he or she is a teenager?

_____

_____

Today's "Bad Mom" moment:

_____

_____

Today's "Best Mom Ever!" moment:

_____

_____

Based on my child's behavior today, I am sure he or she will grow up to be:

☐ A poet—so quiet and thoughtful!

☐ A boxer—so strong and tough!

☐ A political pundit—so loud and fussy!

☐ An Olympic sprinter—always on the go!

☐ A stand-up comedian—so funny and giggly!

☐ Other: _____ because _____

Extra Mom Notes:

_____

_____

_____

_____

_____

_____

_____

_____

Thursday

What's one lie I told my kid today? (That babies come from storks?
That all of the nutrients are in the bread's crust?)

_____

_____

If a TV camera crew followed me around all day, they'd be filming:

☐ A wacky family sitcom, like *Everybody Loves Raymond* or
Modern Family.

☐ A complex workplace drama, like *Grey's Anatomy* or *The Good Wife.*

☐ A cheesy soap opera, like *Days of Our Lives* or *General Hospital.*

☐ A hyperactive talent contest, like *America's Got Talent* or *So You
Think You Can Dance.*

☐ Other: A _____ show, like

_____

The best actor to play my child would be _____,
because: _____

_____

Based on how I feel today, the best actress to play me would be
_____. She would be perfect because:

_____

_____

Extra Mom Notes:

_____

_____

_____

_____

_____

Friday Favorites! DATE

My child's favorite toy this week was _____

This week, my child's favorite friend was _____

If I had to describe this friend in one word, it would be _____
If I had to describe this friend's parents in one word, it would be
_____

The song my child listened to the most this week was
_____

My feelings about this song:
☐ Love it—one of my favorites!
☐ Like it.
☐ Tolerate it—it could be worse, I guess.
☐ Annoyed by it—it's starting to get on my nerves.
☐ Loathe it—it makes my ears bleed.

The food my child asked for the most this week was _____

I ☐ did ☐ didn't   give him or her this food because:
_____
_____

My favorite mom activity is _____ because:
_____
_____

Extra Mom Notes:
_____
_____
_____
_____

Saturday

Who was my parenting role model today? (Inspiration can come from anywhere, including your favorite TV character, your own parents, even the patient clerk at your local grocery store!)

_____

_____

If my child remembers one thing about today, I hope he or she remembers this:

_____

_____

Make Your Own Bedtime Story!

Once upon a time there was a _____ kid. That child had a mom who was really _____.

One day, the mom and the kid went on an adventure. First, they went to _____. There they met a big _____, who taught them both how to _____.

"_____!" said the kid. "This is the best _____ ever!"

Next, the mom and the kid went to _____. They played _____ and won!

"That was _____," said the mom, "but now let's go home."

So the mom and the kid went home and ate _____ for dinner. They brushed their teeth, put on their _____, and went to bed.

Extra Mom Notes:

_____

_____

_____

_____

_____

Sunday

Weekly Look Back

What's one thing that I learned about my child this week?

_____

_____

_____

What's one thing that my child learned about me this week?

_____

_____

_____

What's one thing that I learned about myself?

_____

_____

_____

What's my biggest hope for next week?

_____

_____

_____

Extra Mom Notes:

_____

_____

_____

_____

_____

_____

_____

What was the cutest thing my child did today?

_____

_____

What did my kid smell like today? (Shampoo? Fruit punch? The family dog?)

_____

_____

What did I do today that I never would have done before I was a mom?

_____

_____

How much sleep did I get last night?

☐ **More than 8 hours:** I feel like a Disney princess!

☐ **Between 6 and 8 hours:** A few hits on the ol' snooze button, and I'm good to go.

☐ **Between 3 and 6 hours:** My face is permanently stuck in the yawn position.

☐ **Between 1 and 3 hours:** I now understand how zombies feel.

☐ **Sleep?** Hahaha! HAHAHAHA!

Extra Mom Notes:

_____

_____

_____

_____

_____

_____

_____

Tuesday

DATE

The funniest thing my child did today was:

_____

_____

I ☐ did ☐ didn't laugh because:

_____

_____

What did I do today that made my child laugh?

_____

_____

If I could go back in time, what's one thing that I'd "do over" today?

_____

_____

Today I wished that I was my child's age so that I could

_____

_____ !

The mealtime breakdown:

___% Splattered against the wall   ___% Eaten by my kid

___% Hidden in the napkin   ___% Other: _____

___% Fed to the dog   _____

Extra Mom Notes:

_____

_____

_____

_____

_____

_____

Wednesday

What's one thing my child did today that will embarrass him or her when he or she is a teenager?

_____

_____

Today's "Bad Mom" moment:

_____

_____

Today's "Best Mom Ever!" moment:

_____

_____

Based on my child's behavior today, I am sure he or she will grow up to be:

☐ A poet—so quiet and thoughtful!

☐ A boxer—so strong and tough!

☐ A political pundit—so loud and fussy!

☐ An Olympic sprinter—always on the go!

☐ A stand-up comedian—so funny and giggly!

☐ Other: _____ because _____

Extra Mom Notes:

_____

_____

_____

_____

_____

_____

_____

_____

Thursday

What's one lie I told my kid today? (That babies come from storks?
That all of the nutrients are in the bread's crust?)

_____

_____

If a TV camera crew followed me around all day, they'd be filming:

☐ A wacky family sitcom, like _Everybody Loves Raymond_ or
Modern Family.

☐ A complex workplace drama, like _Grey's Anatomy_ or _The Good Wife._

☐ A cheesy soap opera, like _Days of Our Lives_ or _General Hospital._

☐ A hyperactive talent contest, like _America's Got Talent_ or _So You
Think You Can Dance._

☐ Other: A _____ show, like
_____

The best actor to play my child would be _____,

because: _____

_____

Based on how I feel today, the best actress to play me would be
_____. She would be perfect because:

_____

_____

Extra Mom Notes:

_____

_____

_____

_____

_____

Friday Favorites!

My child's favorite toy this week was _____

This week, my child's favorite friend was _____

If I had to describe this friend in one word, it would be _____
If I had to describe this friend's parents in one word, it would be
_____

The song my child listened to the most this week was
_____

My feelings about this song:
- ☐ Love it—one of my favorites!
- ☐ Like it.
- ☐ Tolerate it—it could be worse, I guess.
- ☐ Annoyed by it—it's starting to get on my nerves.
- ☐ Loathe it—it makes my ears bleed.

The food my child asked for the most this week was _____

I ☐ did ☐ didn't give him or her this food because:
_____
_____

My favorite mom activity is _____ because:
_____
_____

Extra Mom Notes:
_____
_____
_____
_____

Saturday

Who was my parenting role model today? (Inspiration can come from anywhere, including your favorite TV character, your own parents, even the patient clerk at your local grocery store!)

_____

_____

If my child remembers one thing about today, I hope he or she remembers this:

_____

_____

Make Your Own Bedtime Story!

Once upon a time there was a _____ kid. That child had a mom who was really _____.

One day, the mom and the kid went on an adventure. First, they went to _____. There they met a big _____, who taught them both how to _____.

"_____!" said the kid. "This is the best _____ ever!"

Next, the mom and the kid went to _____. They played _____ and won!

"That was _____," said the mom, "but now let's go home."

So the mom and the kid went home and ate _____ for dinner. They brushed their teeth, put on their _____, and went to bed.

Extra Mom Notes:

_____

_____

_____

_____

_____

Weekly Look Back

What's one thing that I learned about my child this week?

_____
_____
_____

What's one thing that my child learned about me this week?

_____
_____
_____

What's one thing that I learned about myself?

_____
_____
_____

What's my biggest hope for next week?

_____
_____
_____

Extra Mom Notes:

_____
_____
_____
_____
_____
_____
_____

Monday

What was the cutest thing my child did today?

_____
_____

What did my kid smell like today? (Shampoo? Fruit punch? The family dog?)

_____
_____

What did I do today that I never would have done before I was a mom?

_____
_____

How much sleep did I get last night?

☐ More than 8 hours: I feel like a Disney princess!

☐ Between 6 and 8 hours: A few hits on the ol' snooze button, and I'm good to go.

☐ Between 3 and 6 hours: My face is permanently stuck in the yawn position.

☐ Between 1 and 3 hours: I now understand how zombies feel.

☐ Sleep? Hahaha! HAHAHAHA!

Extra Mom Notes:

_____
_____
_____
_____
_____
_____
_____

The funniest thing my child did today was:

_____

_____

I ☐ did ☐ didn't laugh because:

_____

_____

What did I do today that made my child laugh?

_____

_____

If I could go back in time, what's one thing that I'd "do over" today?

_____

_____

Today I wished that I was my child's age so that I could

_____

_____!

The mealtime breakdown:

___% Splattered against the wall   ___% Eaten by my kid

___% Hidden in the napkin   ___% Other: _____

___% Fed to the dog   _____

Extra Mom Notes:

_____

_____

_____

_____

_____

_____

Wednesday

DATE

What's one thing my child did today that will embarrass him or her when he or she is a teenager?

_____

_____

Today's "Bad Mom" moment:

_____

_____

Today's "Best Mom Ever!" moment:

_____

_____

Based on my child's behavior today, I am sure he or she will grow up to be:

☐ A poet—so quiet and thoughtful!

☐ A boxer—so strong and tough!

☐ A political pundit—so loud and fussy!

☐ An Olympic sprinter—always on the go!

☐ A stand-up comedian—so funny and giggly!

☐ Other: _____ because _____

Extra Mom Notes:

_____

_____

_____

_____

_____

_____

_____

_____

Thursday

What's one lie I told my kid today? (That babies come from storks? That all of the nutrients are in the bread's crust?)

_____

_____

If a TV camera crew followed me around all day, they'd be filming:

☐ A wacky family sitcom, like *Everybody Loves Raymond* or *Modern Family.*

☐ A complex workplace drama, like *Grey's Anatomy* or *The Good Wife.*

☐ A cheesy soap opera, like *Days of Our Lives* or *General Hospital.*

☐ A hyperactive talent contest, like *America's Got Talent* or *So You Think You Can Dance.*

☐ Other: A _____ show, like

_____

The best actor to play my child would be _____,

because: _____

_____

Based on how I feel today, the best actress to play me would be

_____. She would be perfect because:

_____

_____

Extra Mom Notes:

_____

_____

_____

_____

_____

Friday Favorites! DATE

My child's favorite toy this week was _____

This week, my child's favorite friend was _____

If I had to describe this friend in one word, it would be _____

If I had to describe this friend's parents in one word, it would be

_____

The song my child listened to the most this week was

_____

My feelings about this song:

☐ Love it—one of my favorites!

☐ Like it.

☐ Tolerate it—it could be worse, I guess.

☐ Annoyed by it—it's starting to get on my nerves.

☐ Loathe it—it makes my ears bleed.

The food my child asked for the most this week was _____

I   ☐ did   ☐ didn't   give him or her this food because:

_____

_____

My favorite mom activity is _____ **because:**

_____

_____

Extra Mom Notes:

_____

_____

_____

_____

Saturday

Who was my parenting role model today? (Inspiration can come from anywhere, including your favorite TV character, your own parents, even the patient clerk at your local grocery store!)

_____

_____

If my child remembers one thing about today, I hope he or she remembers this:

_____

_____

Make Your Own Bedtime Story!

Once upon a time there was a _____ kid. That child had a mom who was really _____.

One day, the mom and the kid went on an adventure. First, they went to _____. There they met a big _____, who taught them both how to _____.

"_____!" said the kid. "This is the best _____ ever!"

Next, the mom and the kid went to _____. They played _____ and won!

"That was _____," said the mom, "but now let's go home."

So the mom and the kid went home and ate _____ for dinner. They brushed their teeth, put on their _____, and went to bed.

Extra Mom Notes:

_____

_____

_____

_____

_____

Sunday

Weekly Look Back

What's one thing that I learned about my child this week?

_____
_____
_____

What's one thing that my child learned about me this week?

_____
_____
_____

What's one thing that I learned about myself?

_____
_____
_____

What's my biggest hope for next week?

_____
_____
_____

Extra Mom Notes:

_____
_____
_____
_____
_____
_____
_____

What was the cutest thing my child did today?

_____

_____

**What did my kid smell like today? (Shampoo? Fruit punch?
The family dog?)**

_____

_____

**What did I do today that I never would have done before I was
a mom?**

_____

_____

How much sleep did I get last night?

☐ **More than 8 hours:** I feel like a Disney princess!

☐ **Between 6 and 8 hours:** A few hits on the ol' snooze button, and
I'm good to go.

☐ **Between 3 and 6 hours:** My face is permanently stuck in the yawn
position.

☐ **Between 1 and 3 hours:** I now understand how zombies feel.

☐ **Sleep?** Hahaha! HAHAHAHA!

Extra Mom Notes:

_____

_____

_____

_____

_____

_____

Tuesday

The funniest thing my child did today was:

_____

_____

I ☐ did ☐ didn't laugh because:

_____

_____

What did I do today that made my child laugh?

_____

_____

If I could go back in time, what's one thing that I'd "do over" today?

_____

_____

Today I wished that I was my child's age so that I could

_____

_____ !

The mealtime breakdown:

___% Splattered against the wall   ___% Eaten by my kid

___% Hidden in the napkin   ___% Other: _____

___% Fed to the dog   _____

Extra Mom Notes:

_____

_____

_____

_____

_____

Wednesday

What's one thing my child did today that will embarrass him or her when he or she is a teenager?

_____

_____

Today's "Bad Mom" moment:

_____

_____

Today's "Best Mom Ever!" moment:

_____

_____

Based on my child's behavior today, I am sure he or she will grow up to be:

☐ A poet—so quiet and thoughtful!

☐ A boxer—so strong and tough!

☐ A political pundit—so loud and fussy!

☐ An Olympic sprinter—always on the go!

☐ A stand-up comedian—so funny and giggly!

☐ Other: _____ because _____

Extra Mom Notes:

_____

_____

_____

_____

_____

_____

_____

_____

Thursday

What's one lie I told my kid today? (That babies come from storks?
That all of the nutrients are in the bread's crust?)

_____

_____

If a TV camera crew followed me around all day, they'd be filming:

☐ A wacky family sitcom, like _Everybody Loves Raymond_ or
Modern Family.

☐ A complex workplace drama, like _Grey's Anatomy_ or _The Good Wife._

☐ A cheesy soap opera, like _Days of Our Lives_ or _General Hospital._

☐ A hyperactive talent contest, like _America's Got Talent_ or _So You
Think You Can Dance._

☐ Other: A _____ show, like

_____

The best actor to play my child would be _____,
because: _____

_____

Based on how I feel today, the best actress to play me would be
_____. She would be perfect because:

_____

_____

Extra Mom Notes:

_____

_____

_____

_____

_____

Friday Favorites!

My child's favorite toy this week was _____

This week, my child's favorite friend was _____

If I had to describe this friend in one word, it would be _____

If I had to describe this friend's parents in one word, it would be

_____

The song my child listened to the most this week was

_____

My feelings about this song:

☐ Love it—one of my favorites!

☐ Like it.

☐ Tolerate it—it could be worse, I guess.

☐ Annoyed by it—it's starting to get on my nerves.

☐ Loathe it—it makes my ears bleed.

The food my child asked for the most this week was _____

I ☐ did ☐ didn't give him or her this food because:

_____

_____

My favorite mom activity is _____ because:

_____

_____

Extra Mom Notes:

_____

_____

_____

_____

Saturday

Who was my parenting role model today? (Inspiration can come from anywhere, including your favorite TV character, your own parents, even the patient clerk at your local grocery store!)

_____

_____

If my child remembers one thing about today, I hope he or she remembers this:

_____

_____

Make Your Own Bedtime Story!

Once upon a time there was a _____ kid. That child had a mom who was really _____.

One day, the mom and the kid went on an adventure. First, they went to _____. There they met a big _____, who taught them both how to _____.

"_____!" said the kid. "This is the best _____ ever!"

Next, the mom and the kid went to _____. They played _____ and won!

"That was _____," said the mom, "but now let's go home."

So the mom and the kid went home and ate _____ for dinner. They brushed their teeth, put on their _____, and went to bed.

Extra Mom Notes:

_____

_____

_____

_____

_____

Weekly Look Back

What's one thing that I learned about my child this week?

_____
_____
_____

What's one thing that my child learned about me this week?

_____
_____
_____

What's one thing that I learned about myself?

_____
_____
_____

What's my biggest hope for next week?

_____
_____
_____

Extra Mom Notes:

_____
_____
_____
_____
_____
_____
_____
_____

Monday

What was the cutest thing my child did today?

_____

_____

What did my kid smell like today? (Shampoo? Fruit punch? The family dog?)

_____

_____

What did I do today that I never would have done before I was a mom?

_____

_____

How much sleep did I get last night?

☐ **More than 8 hours:** I feel like a Disney princess!

☐ **Between 6 and 8 hours:** A few hits on the ol' snooze button, and I'm good to go.

☐ **Between 3 and 6 hours:** My face is permanently stuck in the yawn position.

☐ **Between 1 and 3 hours:** I now understand how zombies feel.

☐ **Sleep?** Hahaha! HAHAHAHA!

Extra Mom Notes:

_____

_____

_____

_____

_____

_____

DATE

Tuesday

The funniest thing my child did today was:

_____

_____

I ☐ did ☐ didn't **laugh because:**

_____

_____

What did I do today that made my child laugh?

_____

_____

If I could go back in time, what's one thing that I'd "do over" today?

_____

_____

Today I wished that I was my child's age so that I could

_____

_____!

The mealtime breakdown:

____% Splattered against the wall ____% Eaten by my kid

____% Hidden in the napkin ____% Other: _____

____% Fed to the dog _____

Extra Mom Notes:

_____

_____

_____

_____

_____

Wednesday

What's one thing my child did today that will embarrass him or her when he or she is a teenager?

_____

_____

Today's "Bad Mom" moment:

_____

_____

Today's "Best Mom Ever!" moment:

_____

_____

Based on my child's behavior today, I am sure he or she will grow up to be:

☐ A poet—so quiet and thoughtful!

☐ A boxer—so strong and tough!

☐ A political pundit—so loud and fussy!

☐ An Olympic sprinter—always on the go!

☐ A stand-up comedian—so funny and giggly!

☐ Other: _____ because _____

Extra Mom Notes:

_____

_____

_____

_____

_____

_____

_____

_____

Thursday

What's one lie I told my kid today? (That babies come from storks? That all of the nutrients are in the bread's crust?)

_____

_____

If a TV camera crew followed me around all day, they'd be filming:

☐ A wacky family sitcom, like *Everybody Loves Raymond* or *Modern Family*.

☐ A complex workplace drama, like *Grey's Anatomy* or *The Good Wife*.

☐ A cheesy soap opera, like *Days of Our Lives* or *General Hospital*.

☐ A hyperactive talent contest, like *America's Got Talent* or *So You Think You Can Dance*.

☐ Other: A _____ show, like

_____

The best actor to play my child would be _____,

because: _____

_____

Based on how I feel today, the best actress to play me would be

_____. She would be perfect because:

_____

_____

Extra Mom Notes:

_____

_____

_____

_____

_____

Friday Favorites! DATE

My child's favorite toy this week was _____

This week, my child's favorite friend was _____

If I had to describe this friend in one word, it would be _____
If I had to describe this friend's parents in one word, it would be
_____

The song my child listened to the most this week was
_____

My feelings about this song:
☐ Love it—one of my favorites!
☐ Like it.
☐ Tolerate it—it could be worse, I guess.
☐ Annoyed by it—it's starting to get on my nerves.
☐ Loathe it—it makes my ears bleed.

The food my child asked for the most this week was _____

I ☐ did ☐ didn't give him or her this food because:
_____
_____

My favorite mom activity is _____ because:
_____
_____

Extra Mom Notes:
_____
_____
_____
_____

Saturday

Who was my parenting role model today? (Inspiration can come from anywhere, including your favorite TV character, your own parents, even the patient clerk at your local grocery store!)

_____

_____

If my child remembers one thing about today, I hope he or she remembers this:

_____

_____

Make Your Own Bedtime Story!

Once upon a time there was a _____ kid. That child had a mom who was really _____.

One day, the mom and the kid went on an adventure. First, they went to _____. There they met a big _____, who taught them both how to _____.

"_____!" said the kid. "This is the best _____ ever!"

Next, the mom and the kid went to _____. They played _____ and won!

"That was _____," said the mom, "but now let's go home."

So the mom and the kid went home and ate _____ for dinner. They brushed their teeth, put on their _____, and went to bed.

Extra Mom Notes:

_____

_____

_____

_____

_____

Sunday

Weekly Look Back

What's one thing that I learned about my child this week?

_____

_____

_____

What's one thing that my child learned about me this week?

_____

_____

_____

What's one thing that I learned about myself?

_____

_____

_____

What's my biggest hope for next week?

_____

_____

_____

Extra Mom Notes:

_____

_____

_____

_____

_____

_____

What was the cutest thing my child did today?

_____

_____

What did my kid smell like today? (Shampoo? Fruit punch?
The family dog?)

_____

_____

What did I do today that I never would have done before I was
a mom?

_____

_____

How much sleep did I get last night?

☐ **More than 8 hours:** I feel like a Disney princess!

☐ **Between 6 and 8 hours:** A few hits on the ol' snooze button, and
I'm good to go.

☐ **Between 3 and 6 hours:** My face is permanently stuck in the yawn
position.

☐ **Between 1 and 3 hours:** I now understand how zombies feel.

☐ **Sleep?** Hahaha! HAHAHAHA!

Extra Mom Notes:

_____

_____

_____

_____

_____

_____

Tuesday

The funniest thing my child did today was:

_____

_____

I ☐ did ☐ didn't   laugh because:

_____

_____

What did I do today that made my child laugh?

_____

_____

If I could go back in time, what's one thing that I'd "do over" today?

_____

_____

Today I wished that I was my child's age so that I could

_____

_____ !

The mealtime breakdown:

___% Splattered against the wall   ___% Eaten by my kid

___% Hidden in the napkin   ___% Other: _____

___% Fed to the dog   _____

Extra Mom Notes:

_____

_____

_____

_____

_____

_____

Wednesday

What's one thing my child did today that will embarrass him or her when he or she is a teenager?

_____

_____

Today's "Bad Mom" moment:

_____

_____

Today's "Best Mom Ever!" moment:

_____

_____

Based on my child's behavior today, I am sure he or she will grow up to be:

☐ A poet—so quiet and thoughtful!

☐ A boxer—so strong and tough!

☐ A political pundit—so loud and fussy!

☐ An Olympic sprinter—always on the go!

☐ A stand-up comedian—so funny and giggly!

☐ Other: _____ because _____

Extra Mom Notes:

_____

_____

_____

_____

_____

_____

_____

_____

Thursday

What's one lie I told my kid today? (That babies come from storks?
That all of the nutrients are in the bread's crust?)

_____

_____

If a TV camera crew followed me around all day, they'd be filming:

☐ A wacky family sitcom, like _Everybody Loves Raymond_ or
Modern Family.

☐ A complex workplace drama, like _Grey's Anatomy_ or _The Good Wife._

☐ A cheesy soap opera, like _Days of Our Lives_ or _General Hospital._

☐ A hyperactive talent contest, like _America's Got Talent_ or _So You
Think You Can Dance._

☐ Other: A _____ show, like

_____

The best actor to play my child would be _____,
because: _____

_____

Based on how I feel today, the best actress to play me would be
_____. She would be perfect because:

_____

_____

Extra Mom Notes:

_____

_____

_____

_____

_____

Friday Favorites!

My child's favorite toy this week was _____

This week, my child's favorite friend was _____

If I had to describe this friend in one word, it would be _____
If I had to describe this friend's parents in one word, it would be
_____

The song my child listened to the most this week was
_____

My feelings about this song:
- ☐ Love it—one of my favorites!
- ☐ Like it.
- ☐ Tolerate it—it could be worse, I guess.
- ☐ Annoyed by it—it's starting to get on my nerves.
- ☐ Loathe it—it makes my ears bleed.

The food my child asked for the most this week was _____

I ☐ did ☐ didn't give him or her this food because:
_____
_____

My favorite mom activity is _____ because:
_____
_____

Extra Mom Notes:
_____
_____
_____
_____

Saturday

Who was my parenting role model today? (Inspiration can come from anywhere, including your favorite TV character, your own parents, even the patient clerk at your local grocery store!)

_____

_____

If my child remembers one thing about today, I hope he or she remembers this:

_____

_____

Make Your Own Bedtime Story!

Once upon a time there was a _____ kid. That child had a mom who was really _____.

One day, the mom and the kid went on an adventure. First, they went to _____. There they met a big _____, who taught them both how to _____.

"_____!" said the kid. "This is the best _____ ever!"

Next, the mom and the kid went to _____. They played _____ and won!

"That was _____," said the mom, "but now let's go home."

So the mom and the kid went home and ate _____ for dinner. They brushed their teeth, put on their _____, and went to bed.

Extra Mom Notes:

_____

_____

_____

_____

Weekly Look Back

What's one thing that I learned about my child this week?

_____
_____
_____

What's one thing that my child learned about me this week?

_____
_____
_____

What's one thing that I learned about myself?

_____
_____
_____

What's my biggest hope for next week?

_____
_____
_____

Extra Mom Notes:

_____
_____
_____
_____
_____
_____
_____

Monday

DATE

What was the cutest thing my child did today?

_____

_____

What did my kid smell like today? (Shampoo? Fruit punch?
The family dog?)

_____

_____

What did I do today that I never would have done before I was
a mom?

_____

_____

How much sleep did I get last night?

☐ More than 8 hours: I feel like a Disney princess!

☐ Between 6 and 8 hours: A few hits on the ol' snooze button, and
  I'm good to go.

☐ Between 3 and 6 hours: My face is permanently stuck in the yawn
  position.

☐ Between 1 and 3 hours: I now understand how zombies feel.

☐ Sleep? Hahaha! HAHAHAHA!

Extra Mom Notes:

_____

_____

_____

_____

_____

_____

_____

Tuesday

The funniest thing my child did today was:

_____

_____

I ☐ did ☐ didn't **laugh because:**

_____

_____

What did I do today that made my child laugh?

_____

_____

If I could go back in time, what's one thing that I'd "do over" today?

_____

_____

Today I wished that I was my child's age so that I could

_____

_____!

The mealtime breakdown:

___% Splattered against the wall   ___% Eaten by my kid

___% Hidden in the napkin   ___% Other: _____

___% Fed to the dog   _____

Extra Mom Notes:

_____

_____

_____

_____

_____

_____

Wednesday

What's one thing my child did today that will embarrass him or her when he or she is a teenager?

_____

_____

Today's "Bad Mom" moment:

_____

_____

Today's "Best Mom Ever!" moment:

_____

_____

Based on my child's behavior today, I am sure he or she will grow up to be:

☐ A poet—so quiet and thoughtful!

☐ A boxer—so strong and tough!

☐ A political pundit—so loud and fussy!

☐ An Olympic sprinter—always on the go!

☐ A stand-up comedian—so funny and giggly!

☐ Other: _____ because _____

Extra Mom Notes:

_____

_____

_____

_____

_____

_____

_____

_____

What's one lie I told my kid today? (That babies come from storks?
That all of the nutrients are in the bread's crust?)

_____

_____

If a TV camera crew followed me around all day, they'd be filming:

☐ A wacky family sitcom, like *Everybody Loves Raymond* or
Modern Family.

☐ A complex workplace drama, like *Grey's Anatomy* or *The Good Wife*.

☐ A cheesy soap opera, like *Days of Our Lives* or *General Hospital*.

☐ A hyperactive talent contest, like *America's Got Talent* or *So You
Think You Can Dance*.

☐ Other: A _____ show, like
_____

The best actor to play my child would be _____,
because: _____

_____

Based on how I feel today, the best actress to play me would be
_____. She would be perfect because:

_____

_____

Extra Mom Notes:

_____

_____

_____

_____

_____

Friday Favorites! DATE _____

My child's favorite toy this week was _____

This week, my child's favorite friend was _____

If I had to describe this friend in one word, it would be _____

If I had to describe this friend's parents in one word, it would be

_____

The song my child listened to the most this week was

_____

My feelings about this song:

☐ Love it—one of my favorites!

☐ Like it.

☐ Tolerate it—it could be worse, I guess.

☐ Annoyed by it—it's starting to get on my nerves.

☐ Loathe it—it makes my ears bleed.

The food my child asked for the most this week was _____

I ☐ did ☐ didn't   give him or her this food because:

_____

_____

My favorite mom activity is _____ because:

_____

_____

Extra Mom Notes:

_____

_____

_____

_____

Who was my parenting role model today? (Inspiration can come from anywhere, including your favorite TV character, your own parents, even the patient clerk at your local grocery store!)

_____

_____

If my child remembers one thing about today, I hope he or she remembers this:

_____

_____

Make Your Own Bedtime Story!

Once upon a time there was a _____ kid. That child had a mom who was really _____.

One day, the mom and the kid went on an adventure. First, they went to _____. There they met a big _____, who taught them both how to _____.

"_____!" said the kid. "This is the best _____ ever!"

Next, the mom and the kid went to _____. They played _____ and won!

"That was _____," said the mom, "but now let's go home."

So the mom and the kid went home and ate _____ for dinner.

They brushed their teeth, put on their _____, and went to bed.

Extra Mom Notes:

_____

_____

_____

_____

_____

Sunday

Weekly Look Back

What's one thing that I learned about my child this week?

_____

_____

_____

What's one thing that my child learned about me this week?

_____

_____

_____

What's one thing that I learned about myself?

_____

_____

_____

What's my biggest hope for next week?

_____

_____

_____

Extra Mom Notes:

_____

_____

_____

_____

_____

_____

_____

What was the cutest thing my child did today?

_____

_____

What did my kid smell like today? (Shampoo? Fruit punch? The family dog?)

_____

_____

What did I do today that I never would have done before I was a mom?

_____

_____

How much sleep did I get last night?

☐ **More than 8 hours:** I feel like a Disney princess!

☐ **Between 6 and 8 hours:** A few hits on the ol' snooze button, and I'm good to go.

☐ **Between 3 and 6 hours:** My face is permanently stuck in the yawn position.

☐ **Between 1 and 3 hours:** I now understand how zombies feel.

☐ **Sleep?** Hahaha! HAHAHAHA!

Extra Mom Notes:

_____

_____

_____

_____

_____

_____

_____

Tuesday

DATE

The funniest thing my child did today was:

_____

_____

I ☐ did ☐ didn't laugh because:

_____

_____

What did I do today that made my child laugh?

_____

_____

If I could go back in time, what's one thing that I'd "do over" today?

_____

_____

Today I wished that I was my child's age so that I could

_____

_____ !

The mealtime breakdown:

___% Splattered against the wall   ___% Eaten by my kid

___% Hidden in the napkin   ___% Other: _____

___% Fed to the dog   _____

Extra Mom Notes:

_____

_____

_____

_____

_____

_____

Wednesday

What's one thing my child did today that will embarrass him or her when he or she is a teenager?

_____
_____

Today's "Bad Mom" moment:

_____
_____

Today's "Best Mom Ever!" moment:

_____
_____

Based on my child's behavior today, I am sure he or she will grow up to be:

☐ A poet—so quiet and thoughtful!
☐ A boxer—so strong and tough!
☐ A political pundit—so loud and fussy!
☐ An Olympic sprinter—always on the go!
☐ A stand-up comedian—so funny and giggly!
☐ Other: _____ because _____

Extra Mom Notes:

_____
_____
_____
_____
_____
_____
_____
_____

Thursday

What's one lie I told my kid today? (That babies come from storks? That all of the nutrients are in the bread's crust?)

_____

_____

If a TV camera crew followed me around all day, they'd be filming:

☐ A wacky family sitcom, like *Everybody Loves Raymond* or *Modern Family.*

☐ A complex workplace drama, like *Grey's Anatomy* or *The Good Wife.*

☐ A cheesy soap opera, like *Days of Our Lives* or *General Hospital.*

☐ A hyperactive talent contest, like *America's Got Talent* or *So You Think You Can Dance.*

☐ Other: A _____ show, like

_____

The best actor to play my child would be _____,

because: _____

_____

Based on how I feel today, the best actress to play me would be

_____. She would be perfect because:

_____

_____

Extra Mom Notes:

_____

_____

_____

_____

_____

My child's favorite toy this week was _____

This week, my child's favorite friend was _____

If I had to describe this friend in one word, it would be _____
If I had to describe this friend's parents in one word, it would be

_____

The song my child listened to the most this week was

_____

My feelings about this song:
☐ Love it—one of my favorites!
☐ Like it.
☐ Tolerate it—it could be worse, I guess.
☐ Annoyed by it—it's starting to get on my nerves.
☐ Loathe it—it makes my ears bleed.

The food my child asked for the most this week was _____

I ☐ did ☐ didn't give him or her this food because:

_____
_____

My favorite mom activity is _____ **because:**

_____
_____

Extra Mom Notes:

_____
_____
_____
_____

Saturday

Who was my parenting role model today? (Inspiration can come from anywhere, including your favorite TV character, your own parents, even the patient clerk at your local grocery store!)

_____

_____

If my child remembers one thing about today, I hope he or she remembers this:

_____

_____

Make Your Own Bedtime Story!

Once upon a time there was a _____ kid. That child had a mom who was really _____.

One day, the mom and the kid went on an adventure. First, they went to _____. There they met a big _____, who taught them both how to _____.

"_____!" said the kid. "This is the best _____ ever!"

Next, the mom and the kid went to _____. They played _____ and won!

"That was _____," said the mom, "but now let's go home."

So the mom and the kid went home and ate _____ for dinner. They brushed their teeth, put on their _____, and went to bed.

Extra Mom Notes:

_____

_____

_____

_____

_____

Weekly Look Back

What's one thing that I learned about my child this week?

_____
_____
_____

What's one thing that my child learned about me this week?

_____
_____
_____

What's one thing that I learned about myself?

_____
_____
_____

What's my biggest hope for next week?

_____
_____
_____

Extra Mom Notes:

_____
_____
_____
_____
_____
_____
_____

Monday

What was the cutest thing my child did today?

_____

_____

What did my kid smell like today? (Shampoo? Fruit punch? The family dog?)

_____

_____

What did I do today that I never would have done before I was a mom?

_____

_____

How much sleep did I get last night?

☐ More than 8 hours: I feel like a Disney princess!

☐ Between 6 and 8 hours: A few hits on the ol' snooze button, and I'm good to go.

☐ Between 3 and 6 hours: My face is permanently stuck in the yawn position.

☐ Between 1 and 3 hours: I now understand how zombies feel.

☐ Sleep? Hahaha! HAHAHAHA!

Extra Mom Notes:

_____

_____

_____

_____

_____

_____

_____

Tuesday

The funniest thing my child did today was:

_____

_____

I ☐ did ☐ didn't laugh because:

_____

_____

What did I do today that made my child laugh?

_____

_____

If I could go back in time, what's one thing that I'd "do over" today?

_____

_____

Today I wished that I was my child's age so that I could

_____

_____ !

The mealtime breakdown:

____% Splattered against the wall   ____% Eaten by my kid

____% Hidden in the napkin   ____% Other: _____

____% Fed to the dog   _____

Extra Mom Notes:

_____

_____

_____

_____

_____

Wednesday

What's one thing my child did today that will embarrass him or her when he or she is a teenager?

_____

_____

Today's "Bad Mom" moment:

_____

_____

Today's "Best Mom Ever!" moment:

_____

_____

Based on my child's behavior today, I am sure he or she will grow up to be:

☐ A poet—so quiet and thoughtful!

☐ A boxer—so strong and tough!

☐ A political pundit—so loud and fussy!

☐ An Olympic sprinter—always on the go!

☐ A stand-up comedian—so funny and giggly!

☐ Other: _____ because _____

Extra Mom Notes:

_____

_____

_____

_____

_____

_____

_____

_____

Thursday

What's one lie I told my kid today? (That babies come from storks? That all of the nutrients are in the bread's crust?)

_____

_____

If a TV camera crew followed me around all day, they'd be filming:

☐ A wacky family sitcom, like *Everybody Loves Raymond* or *Modern Family.*

☐ A complex workplace drama, like *Grey's Anatomy* or *The Good Wife.*

☐ A cheesy soap opera, like *Days of Our Lives* or *General Hospital.*

☐ A hyperactive talent contest, like *America's Got Talent* or *So You Think You Can Dance.*

☐ Other: A _____ show, like

_____

The best actor to play my child would be _____,

because: _____

_____

Based on how I feel today, the best actress to play me would be

_____. She would be perfect because:

_____

_____

Extra Mom Notes:

_____

_____

_____

_____

_____

Friday Favorites! DATE

My child's favorite toy this week was _____

This week, my child's favorite friend was _____

If I had to describe this friend in one word, it would be _____

If I had to describe this friend's parents in one word, it would be

_____

The song my child listened to the most this week was

_____

My feelings about this song:

☐ Love it—one of my favorites!

☐ Like it.

☐ Tolerate it—it could be worse, I guess.

☐ Annoyed by it—it's starting to get on my nerves.

☐ Loathe it—it makes my ears bleed.

The food my child asked for the most this week was _____

I ☐ did ☐ didn't give him or her this food because:

_____

_____

My favorite mom activity is _____ because:

_____

_____

Extra Mom Notes:

_____

_____

_____

_____

Saturday

Who was my parenting role model today? (Inspiration can come from anywhere, including your favorite TV character, your own parents, even the patient clerk at your local grocery store!)

_____

_____

If my child remembers one thing about today, I hope he or she remembers this:

_____

_____

Make Your Own Bedtime Story!

Once upon a time there was a _____ kid. That child had a mom who was really _____.

One day, the mom and the kid went on an adventure. First, they went to _____. There they met a big _____, who taught them both how to _____.

"_____!" said the kid. "This is the best _____ ever!"

Next, the mom and the kid went to _____. They played _____ and won!

"That was _____," said the mom, "but now let's go home."

So the mom and the kid went home and ate _____ for dinner. They brushed their teeth, put on their _____, and went to bed.

Extra Mom Notes:

_____

_____

_____

_____

_____

Sunday

Weekly Look Back

What's one thing that I learned about my child this week?

_____
_____
_____

What's one thing that my child learned about me this week?

_____
_____
_____

What's one thing that I learned about myself?

_____
_____
_____

What's my biggest hope for next week?

_____
_____
_____

Extra Mom Notes:

_____
_____
_____
_____
_____
_____
_____

What was the cutest thing my child did today?

_____

_____

What did my kid smell like today? (Shampoo? Fruit punch? The family dog?)

_____

_____

What did I do today that I never would have done before I was a mom?

_____

_____

How much sleep did I get last night?

☐ **More than 8 hours:** I feel like a Disney princess!

☐ **Between 6 and 8 hours:** A few hits on the ol' snooze button, and I'm good to go.

☐ **Between 3 and 6 hours:** My face is permanently stuck in the yawn position.

☐ **Between 1 and 3 hours:** I now understand how zombies feel.

☐ **Sleep?** Hahaha! HAHAHAHA!

Extra Mom Notes:

_____

_____

_____

_____

_____

_____

_____

Tuesday

DATE

The funniest thing my child did today was:

_____

_____

I ☐ did ☐ didn't   laugh because:

_____

_____

What did I do today that made my child laugh?

_____

_____

If I could go back in time, what's one thing that I'd "do over" today?

_____

_____

Today I wished that I was my child's age so that I could

_____

_____!

The mealtime breakdown:

___% Splattered against the wall   ___% Eaten by my kid

___% Hidden in the napkin   ___% Other: _____

___% Fed to the dog   _____

Extra Mom Notes:

_____

_____

_____

_____

_____

What's one thing my child did today that will embarrass him or her when he or she is a teenager?

_____
_____

Today's "Bad Mom" moment:

_____
_____

Today's "Best Mom Ever!" moment:

_____
_____

Based on my child's behavior today, I am sure he or she will grow up to be:

☐ A poet—so quiet and thoughtful!

☐ A boxer—so strong and tough!

☐ A political pundit—so loud and fussy!

☐ An Olympic sprinter—always on the go!

☐ A stand-up comedian—so funny and giggly!

☐ Other: _____ because _____

Extra Mom Notes:

_____
_____
_____
_____
_____
_____
_____
_____
_____

Thursday

DATE

What's one lie I told my kid today? (That babies come from storks? That all of the nutrients are in the bread's crust?)

_____

_____

If a TV camera crew followed me around all day, they'd be filming:

☐ A wacky family sitcom, like _Everybody Loves Raymond_ or _Modern Family._

☐ A complex workplace drama, like _Grey's Anatomy_ or _The Good Wife._

☐ A cheesy soap opera, like _Days of Our Lives_ or _General Hospital._

☐ A hyperactive talent contest, like _America's Got Talent_ or _So You Think You Can Dance._

☐ Other: A _____ show, like

_____

The best actor to play my child would be _____,

because: _____

_____

Based on how I feel today, the best actress to play me would be

_____. She would be perfect because:

_____

_____

Extra Mom Notes:

_____

_____

_____

_____

_____

Friday Favorites!

My child's favorite toy this week was _____

This week, my child's favorite friend was _____

If I had to describe this friend in one word, it would be _____

If I had to describe this friend's parents in one word, it would be

_____

The song my child listened to the most this week was

_____

My feelings about this song:

☐ Love it—one of my favorites!

☐ Like it.

☐ Tolerate it—it could be worse, I guess.

☐ Annoyed by it—it's starting to get on my nerves.

☐ Loathe it—it makes my ears bleed.

The food my child asked for the most this week was _____

I ☐ did ☐ didn't give him or her this food because:

_____

_____

My favorite mom activity is _____ because:

_____

_____

Extra Mom Notes:

_____

_____

_____

_____

Saturday

Who was my parenting role model today? (Inspiration can come from anywhere, including your favorite TV character, your own parents, even the patient clerk at your local grocery store!)

_____

_____

If my child remembers one thing about today, I hope he or she remembers this:

_____

_____

Make Your Own Bedtime Story!

Once upon a time there was a _____ kid. That child had a mom who was really _____.

One day, the mom and the kid went on an adventure. First, they went to _____. There they met a big _____, who taught them both how to _____.

"_____!" said the kid. "This is the best _____ ever!"

Next, the mom and the kid went to _____. They played _____ and won!

"That was _____," said the mom, "but now let's go home."

So the mom and the kid went home and ate _____ for dinner. They brushed their teeth, put on their _____, and went to bed.

Extra Mom Notes:

_____

_____

_____

_____

_____

Weekly Look Back

What's one thing that I learned about my child this week?

_____

_____

_____

What's one thing that my child learned about me this week?

_____

_____

_____

What's one thing that I learned about myself?

_____

_____

_____

What's my biggest hope for next week?

_____

_____

_____

Extra Mom Notes:

_____

_____

_____

_____

_____

_____

_____

Monday

What was the cutest thing my child did today?

_____

_____

What did my kid smell like today? (Shampoo? Fruit punch?
The family dog?)

_____

_____

What did I do today that I never would have done before I was
a mom?

_____

_____

How much sleep did I get last night?

☐ More than 8 hours: I feel like a Disney princess!

☐ Between 6 and 8 hours: A few hits on the ol' snooze button, and
I'm good to go.

☐ Between 3 and 6 hours: My face is permanently stuck in the yawn
position.

☐ Between 1 and 3 hours: I now understand how zombies feel.

☐ Sleep? Hahaha! HAHAHAHA!

Extra Mom Notes:

_____

_____

_____

_____

_____

_____

Tuesday

The funniest thing my child did today was:

_____

_____

I ☐ **did** ☐ **didn't laugh because:**

_____

_____

What did I do today that made my child laugh?

_____

_____

If I could go back in time, what's one thing that I'd "do over" today?

_____

_____

Today I wished that I was my child's age so that I could

_____

_____!

The mealtime breakdown:

___% Splattered against the wall   ___% Eaten by my kid

___% Hidden in the napkin   ___% Other: _____

___% Fed to the dog   _____

Extra Mom Notes:

_____

_____

_____

_____

_____

_____

Wednesday

What's one thing my child did today that will embarrass him or her when he or she is a teenager?

_____

_____

Today's "Bad Mom" moment:

_____

_____

Today's "Best Mom Ever!" moment:

_____

_____

Based on my child's behavior today, I am sure he or she will grow up to be:

☐ A poet—so quiet and thoughtful!

☐ A boxer—so strong and tough!

☐ A political pundit—so loud and fussy!

☐ An Olympic sprinter—always on the go!

☐ A stand-up comedian—so funny and giggly!

☐ Other: _____ because _____

Extra Mom Notes:

_____

_____

_____

_____

_____

_____

_____

_____

What's one lie I told my kid today? (That babies come from storks? That all of the nutrients are in the bread's crust?)

_____

_____

If a TV camera crew followed me around all day, they'd be filming:

☐ A wacky family sitcom, like *Everybody Loves Raymond* or *Modern Family*.

☐ A complex workplace drama, like *Grey's Anatomy* or *The Good Wife*.

☐ A cheesy soap opera, like *Days of Our Lives* or *General Hospital*.

☐ A hyperactive talent contest, like *America's Got Talent* or *So You Think You Can Dance.*

☐ Other: A _____ show, like

_____

The best actor to play my child would be _____,
because: _____

_____

Based on how I feel today, the best actress to play me would be
_____. She would be perfect because:

_____

_____

Extra Mom Notes:

_____

_____

_____

_____

_____

Friday Favorites! DATE

My child's favorite toy this week was _____

This week, my child's favorite friend was _____

If I had to describe this friend in one word, it would be _____
If I had to describe this friend's parents in one word, it would be
_____

The song my child listened to the most this week was
_____

My feelings about this song:
- ☐ Love it—one of my favorites!
- ☐ Like it.
- ☐ Tolerate it—it could be worse, I guess.
- ☐ Annoyed by it—it's starting to get on my nerves.
- ☐ Loathe it—it makes my ears bleed.

The food my child asked for the most this week was _____

I ☐ did ☐ didn't give him or her this food because:
_____
_____

My favorite mom activity is _____ because:
_____
_____

Extra Mom Notes:
_____
_____
_____
_____

Who was my parenting role model today? (Inspiration can come from anywhere, including your favorite TV character, your own parents, even the patient clerk at your local grocery store!)

_____

_____

If my child remembers one thing about today, I hope he or she remembers this:

_____

_____

Make Your Own Bedtime Story!

Once upon a time there was a _____ kid. That child had a mom who was really _____.

One day, the mom and the kid went on an adventure. First, they went to _____. There they met a big _____, who taught them both how to _____.

"_____!" said the kid. "This is the best _____ ever!"

Next, the mom and the kid went to _____. They played _____ and won!

"That was _____," said the mom, "but now let's go home."

So the mom and the kid went home and ate _____ for dinner.

They brushed their teeth, put on their _____, and went to bed.

Extra Mom Notes:

_____

_____

_____

_____

_____

Sunday

Weekly Look Back

What's one thing that I learned about my child this week?

_____
_____
_____

What's one thing that my child learned about me this week?

_____
_____
_____

What's one thing that I learned about myself?

_____
_____
_____

What's my biggest hope for next week?

_____
_____
_____

Extra Mom Notes:

_____
_____
_____
_____
_____
_____
_____

Monday

What was the cutest thing my child did today?

_____

_____

What did my kid smell like today? (Shampoo? Fruit punch? The family dog?)

_____

_____

What did I do today that I never would have done before I was a mom?

_____

_____

How much sleep did I get last night?

☐ **More than 8 hours:** I feel like a Disney princess!

☐ **Between 6 and 8 hours:** A few hits on the ol' snooze button, and I'm good to go.

☐ **Between 3 and 6 hours:** My face is permanently stuck in the yawn position.

☐ **Between 1 and 3 hours:** I now understand how zombies feel.

☐ **Sleep?** Hahaha! HAHAHAHA!

Extra Mom Notes:

_____

_____

_____

_____

_____

_____

Tuesday

The funniest thing my child did today was:

_____

_____

I ☐ did ☐ didn't laugh because:

_____

_____

What did I do today that made my child laugh?

_____

_____

If I could go back in time, what's one thing that I'd "do over" today?

_____

_____

Today I wished that I was my child's age so that I could

_____

_____!

The mealtime breakdown:

___% Splattered against the wall   ___% Eaten by my kid

___% Hidden in the napkin   ___% Other: _____

___% Fed to the dog   _____

Extra Mom Notes:

_____

_____

_____

_____

_____

Wednesday

What's one thing my child did today that will embarrass him or her when he or she is a teenager?

_____

_____

Today's "Bad Mom" moment:

_____

_____

Today's "Best Mom Ever!" moment:

_____

_____

Based on my child's behavior today, I am sure he or she will grow up to be:

☐ A poet—so quiet and thoughtful!

☐ A boxer—so strong and tough!

☐ A political pundit—so loud and fussy!

☐ An Olympic sprinter—always on the go!

☐ A stand-up comedian—so funny and giggly!

☐ Other: _____ because _____

Extra Mom Notes:

_____

_____

_____

_____

_____

_____

_____

_____

Thursday

DATE

What's one lie I told my kid today? (That babies come from storks?
That all of the nutrients are in the bread's crust?)

_____

_____

If a TV camera crew followed me around all day, they'd be filming:

☐ A wacky family sitcom, like _Everybody Loves Raymond_ or
Modern Family.

☐ A complex workplace drama, like _Grey's Anatomy_ or _The Good Wife._

☐ A cheesy soap opera, like _Days of Our Lives_ or _General Hospital._

☐ A hyperactive talent contest, like _America's Got Talent_ or _So You
Think You Can Dance._

☐ Other: A _____ show, like
_____

The best actor to play my child would be _____,
because: _____

_____

Based on how I feel today, the best actress to play me would be
_____. She would be perfect because:

_____

_____

Extra Mom Notes:

_____

_____

_____

_____

_____

Friday Favorites!

My child's favorite toy this week was _____

This week, my child's favorite friend was _____

If I had to describe this friend in one word, it would be _____

If I had to describe this friend's parents in one word, it would be

_____

The song my child listened to the most this week was

_____

My feelings about this song:

☐ Love it—one of my favorites!

☐ Like it.

☐ Tolerate it—it could be worse, I guess.

☐ Annoyed by it—it's starting to get on my nerves.

☐ Loathe it—it makes my ears bleed.

The food my child asked for the most this week was _____

I ☐ did ☐ didn't give him or her this food because:

_____

_____

My favorite mom activity is _____ because:

_____

_____

Extra Mom Notes:

_____

_____

_____

_____

Saturday

Who was my parenting role model today? (Inspiration can come from anywhere, including your favorite TV character, your own parents, even the patient clerk at your local grocery store!)

_____

_____

If my child remembers one thing about today, I hope he or she remembers this:

_____

_____

Make Your Own Bedtime Story!

Once upon a time there was a _____ kid. That child had a mom who was really _____.

One day, the mom and the kid went on an adventure. First, they went to _____. There they met a big _____, who taught them both how to _____.

"_____!" said the kid. "This is the best _____ ever!"

Next, the mom and the kid went to _____. They played _____ and won!

"That was _____," said the mom, "but now let's go home."

So the mom and the kid went home and ate _____ for dinner. They brushed their teeth, put on their _____, and went to bed.

Extra Mom Notes:

_____

_____

_____

_____

_____

Weekly Look Back

What's one thing that I learned about my child this week?

_____
_____
_____

What's one thing that my child learned about me this week?

_____
_____
_____

What's one thing that I learned about myself?

_____
_____
_____

What's my biggest hope for next week?

_____
_____
_____

Extra Mom Notes:

_____
_____
_____
_____
_____
_____
_____

Monday

DATE

What was the cutest thing my child did today?

_____

_____

What did my kid smell like today? (Shampoo? Fruit punch? The family dog?)

_____

_____

What did I do today that I never would have done before I was a mom?

_____

_____

How much sleep did I get last night?

☐ **More than 8 hours:** I feel like a Disney princess!

☐ **Between 6 and 8 hours:** A few hits on the ol' snooze button, and I'm good to go.

☐ **Between 3 and 6 hours:** My face is permanently stuck in the yawn position.

☐ **Between 1 and 3 hours:** I now understand how zombies feel.

☐ **Sleep?** Hahaha! HAHAHAHA!

Extra Mom Notes:

_____

_____

_____

_____

_____

_____

Tuesday

The funniest thing my child did today was:

_____

_____

I ☐ did ☐ didn't **laugh because:**

_____

_____

What did I do today that made my child laugh?

_____

_____

If I could go back in time, what's one thing that I'd "do over" today?

_____

_____

Today I wished that I was my child's age so that I could

_____

_____ !

The mealtime breakdown:

____% Splattered against the wall ____% Eaten by my kid

____% Hidden in the napkin ____% Other: _____

____% Fed to the dog _____

Extra Mom Notes:

_____

_____

_____

_____

_____

_____

Wednesday

What's one thing my child did today that will embarrass him or her when he or she is a teenager?

_____

_____

Today's "Bad Mom" moment:

_____

_____

Today's "Best Mom Ever!" moment:

_____

_____

Based on my child's behavior today, I am sure he or she will grow up to be:

☐ A poet—so quiet and thoughtful!

☐ A boxer—so strong and tough!

☐ A political pundit—so loud and fussy!

☐ An Olympic sprinter—always on the go!

☐ A stand-up comedian—so funny and giggly!

☐ Other: _____ because _____

Extra Mom Notes:

_____

_____

_____

_____

_____

_____

_____

Thursday

What's one lie I told my kid today? (That babies come from storks? That all of the nutrients are in the bread's crust?)

_____

_____

If a TV camera crew followed me around all day, they'd be filming:

☐ A wacky family sitcom, like _Everybody Loves Raymond_ or _Modern Family._

☐ A complex workplace drama, like _Grey's Anatomy_ or _The Good Wife._

☐ A cheesy soap opera, like _Days of Our Lives_ or _General Hospital._

☐ A hyperactive talent contest, like _America's Got Talent_ or _So You Think You Can Dance._

☐ Other: A _____ show, like

_____

The best actor to play my child would be _____,

because: _____

_____

Based on how I feel today, the best actress to play me would be

_____. She would be perfect because:

_____

_____

Extra Mom Notes:

_____

_____

_____

_____

_____

Friday Favorites! DATE _____

My child's favorite toy this week was _____

This week, my child's favorite friend was _____

If I had to describe this friend in one word, it would be _____
If I had to describe this friend's parents in one word, it would be
_____

The song my child listened to the most this week was
_____

My feelings about this song:
☐ Love it—one of my favorites!
☐ Like it.
☐ Tolerate it—it could be worse, I guess.
☐ Annoyed by it—it's starting to get on my nerves.
☐ Loathe it—it makes my ears bleed.

The food my child asked for the most this week was _____

I ☐ did ☐ didn't give him or her this food because:
_____
_____

My favorite mom activity is _____ because:
_____
_____

Extra Mom Notes:
_____
_____
_____
_____

Saturday

Who was my parenting role model today? (Inspiration can come from anywhere, including your favorite TV character, your own parents, even the patient clerk at your local grocery store!)

_____

_____

If my child remembers one thing about today, I hope he or she remembers this:

_____

_____

Make Your Own Bedtime Story!

Once upon a time there was a _____ kid. That child had a mom who was really _____.

One day, the mom and the kid went on an adventure. First, they went to _____. There they met a big _____, who taught them both how to _____.

"_____!" said the kid. "This is the best _____ ever!"

Next, the mom and the kid went to _____. They played _____ and won!

"That was _____," said the mom, "but now let's go home."

So the mom and the kid went home and ate _____ for dinner. They brushed their teeth, put on their _____, and went to bed.

Extra Mom Notes:

_____

_____

_____

_____

_____

Sunday

Weekly Look Back

What's one thing that I learned about my child this week?

_____
_____
_____

What's one thing that my child learned about me this week?

_____
_____
_____

What's one thing that I learned about myself?

_____
_____
_____

What's my biggest hope for next week?

_____
_____
_____

Extra Mom Notes:

_____
_____
_____
_____
_____
_____
_____

Monday

What was the cutest thing my child did today?

_____

_____

What did my kid smell like today? (Shampoo? Fruit punch? The family dog?)

_____

_____

What did I do today that I never would have done before I was a mom?

_____

_____

How much sleep did I get last night?

☐ **More than 8 hours:** I feel like a Disney princess!

☐ **Between 6 and 8 hours:** A few hits on the ol' snooze button, and I'm good to go.

☐ **Between 3 and 6 hours:** My face is permanently stuck in the yawn position.

☐ **Between 1 and 3 hours:** I now understand how zombies feel.

☐ **Sleep?** Hahaha! HAHAHAHA!

Extra Mom Notes:

_____

_____

_____

_____

_____

_____

Tuesday

DATE

The funniest thing my child did today was:

_____

_____

I ☐ did ☐ didn't laugh because:

_____

_____

What did I do today that made my child laugh?

_____

_____

If I could go back in time, what's one thing that I'd "do over" today?

_____

_____

Today I wished that I was my child's age so that I could

_____

_____!

The mealtime breakdown:

___% Splattered against the wall   ___% Eaten by my kid

___% Hidden in the napkin   ___% Other: _____

___% Fed to the dog   _____

Extra Mom Notes:

_____

_____

_____

_____

_____

Wednesday

What's one thing my child did today that will embarrass him or her when he or she is a teenager?

_____

_____

Today's "Bad Mom" moment:

_____

_____

Today's "Best Mom Ever!" moment:

_____

_____

Based on my child's behavior today, I am sure he or she will grow up to be:

☐ A poet—so quiet and thoughtful!

☐ A boxer—so strong and tough!

☐ A political pundit—so loud and fussy!

☐ An Olympic sprinter—always on the go!

☐ A stand-up comedian—so funny and giggly!

☐ Other: _____ because _____

Extra Mom Notes:

_____

_____

_____

_____

_____

_____

_____

_____

Thursday

What's one lie I told my kid today? (That babies come from storks?
That all of the nutrients are in the bread's crust?)

_____

_____

If a TV camera crew followed me around all day, they'd be filming:

☐ A wacky family sitcom, like _Everybody Loves Raymond_ or
Modern Family.

☐ A complex workplace drama, like _Grey's Anatomy_ or _The Good Wife._

☐ A cheesy soap opera, like _Days of Our Lives_ or _General Hospital._

☐ A hyperactive talent contest, like _America's Got Talent_ or _So You
Think You Can Dance._

☐ Other: A _____ show, like
_____

The best actor to play my child would be _____,
because: _____

_____

Based on how I feel today, the best actress to play me would be
_____. She would be perfect because:

_____

_____

Extra Mom Notes:

_____

_____

_____

_____

_____

Friday Favorites!

My child's favorite toy this week was _____

This week, my child's favorite friend was _____

If I had to describe this friend in one word, it would be _____
If I had to describe this friend's parents in one word, it would be

_____

The song my child listened to the most this week was

_____

My feelings about this song:

☐ Love it—one of my favorites!
☐ Like it.
☐ Tolerate it—it could be worse, I guess.
☐ Annoyed by it—it's starting to get on my nerves.
☐ Loathe it—it makes my ears bleed.

The food my child asked for the most this week was _____

I   ☐ did   ☐ didn't   give him or her this food because:

_____
_____

My favorite mom activity is _____ because:

_____
_____

Extra Mom Notes:

_____
_____
_____
_____

Saturday

Who was my parenting role model today? (Inspiration can come from anywhere, including your favorite TV character, your own parents, even the patient clerk at your local grocery store!)

_____

_____

If my child remembers one thing about today, I hope he or she remembers this:

_____

_____

Make Your Own Bedtime Story!

Once upon a time there was a _____ kid. That child had a mom who was really _____.

One day, the mom and the kid went on an adventure. First, they went to _____. There they met a big _____, who taught them both how to _____.

"_____!" said the kid. "This is the best _____ ever!"

Next, the mom and the kid went to _____. They played _____ and won!

"That was _____," said the mom, "but now let's go home."

So the mom and the kid went home and ate _____ for dinner. They brushed their teeth, put on their _____, and went to bed.

Extra Mom Notes:

_____

_____

_____

_____

_____

Sunday

Weekly Look Back

What's one thing that I learned about my child this week?

_____
_____
_____

What's one thing that my child learned about me this week?

_____
_____
_____

What's one thing that I learned about myself?

_____
_____
_____

What's my biggest hope for next week?

_____
_____
_____

Extra Mom Notes:

_____
_____
_____
_____
_____
_____
_____

Monday

What was the cutest thing my child did today?

_____

_____

What did my kid smell like today? (Shampoo? Fruit punch? The family dog?)

_____

_____

What did I do today that I never would have done before I was a mom?

_____

_____

How much sleep did I get last night?

☐ **More than 8 hours:** I feel like a Disney princess!

☐ **Between 6 and 8 hours:** A few hits on the ol' snooze button, and I'm good to go.

☐ **Between 3 and 6 hours:** My face is permanently stuck in the yawn position.

☐ **Between 1 and 3 hours:** I now understand how zombies feel.

☐ **Sleep?** Hahaha! HAHAHAHA!

Extra Mom Notes:

_____

_____

_____

_____

_____

_____

_____

The funniest thing my child did today was:

_____

_____

I ☐ did ☐ didn't laugh because:

_____

_____

What did I do today that made my child laugh?

_____

_____

If I could go back in time, what's one thing that I'd "do over" today?

_____

_____

Today I wished that I was my child's age so that I could

_____

_____!

The mealtime breakdown:

____% Splattered against the wall   ____% Eaten by my kid

____% Hidden in the napkin   ____% Other: _____

____% Fed to the dog   _____

Extra Mom Notes:

_____

_____

_____

_____

_____

Wednesday

What's one thing my child did today that will embarrass him or her when he or she is a teenager?

_____

_____

Today's "Bad Mom" moment:

_____

_____

Today's "Best Mom Ever!" moment:

_____

_____

Based on my child's behavior today, I am sure he or she will grow up to be:

☐ A poet—so quiet and thoughtful!

☐ A boxer—so strong and tough!

☐ A political pundit—so loud and fussy!

☐ An Olympic sprinter—always on the go!

☐ A stand-up comedian—so funny and giggly!

☐ Other: _____ because _____

Extra Mom Notes:

_____

_____

_____

_____

_____

_____

_____

Thursday

What's one lie I told my kid today? (That babies come from storks?
That all of the nutrients are in the bread's crust?)

_____

_____

If a TV camera crew followed me around all day, they'd be filming:

☐ **A wacky family sitcom,** like *Everybody Loves Raymond* or
  Modern Family.

☐ **A complex workplace drama,** like *Grey's Anatomy* or *The Good Wife.*

☐ **A cheesy soap opera,** like *Days of Our Lives* or *General Hospital.*

☐ **A hyperactive talent contest,** like *America's Got Talent* or *So You
  Think You Can Dance.*

☐ **Other:** A _____ show, like

_____

The best actor to play my child would be _____,

because: _____

_____

Based on how I feel today, the best actress to play me would be

_____. **She would be perfect because:**

_____

_____

Extra Mom Notes:

_____

_____

_____

_____

_____

Friday Favorites! DATE

My child's favorite toy this week was _____

This week, my child's favorite friend was _____

If I had to describe this friend in one word, it would be _____
If I had to describe this friend's parents in one word, it would be
_____

The song my child listened to the most this week was
_____

My feelings about this song:
☐ Love it—one of my favorites!
☐ Like it.
☐ Tolerate it—it could be worse, I guess.
☐ Annoyed by it—it's starting to get on my nerves.
☐ Loathe it—it makes my ears bleed.

The food my child asked for the most this week was _____

I ☐ did ☐ didn't give him or her this food because:
_____
_____

My favorite mom activity is _____ because:
_____
_____

Extra Mom Notes:
_____
_____
_____
_____

Who was my parenting role model today? (Inspiration can come from anywhere, including your favorite TV character, your own parents, even the patient clerk at your local grocery store!)

_____

_____

If my child remembers one thing about today, I hope he or she remembers this:

_____

_____

Make Your Own Bedtime Story!

Once upon a time there was a _____ kid. That child had a mom who was really _____.

One day, the mom and the kid went on an adventure. First, they went to _____. There they met a big _____, who taught them both how to _____.

"_____!" said the kid. "This is the best _____ ever!" Next, the mom and the kid went to _____. They played _____ and won!

"That was _____," said the mom, "but now let's go home." So the mom and the kid went home and ate _____ for dinner. They brushed their teeth, put on their _____, and went to bed.

Extra Mom Notes:

_____

_____

_____

_____

_____

Sunday

Weekly Look Back

What's one thing that I learned about my child this week?

_____
_____
_____

What's one thing that my child learned about me this week?

_____
_____
_____

What's one thing that I learned about myself?

_____
_____
_____

What's my biggest hope for next week?

_____
_____
_____

Extra Mom Notes:

_____
_____
_____
_____
_____
_____
_____

What was the cutest thing my child did today?

_____

_____

What did my kid smell like today? (Shampoo? Fruit punch?
The family dog?)

_____

_____

What did I do today that I never would have done before I was
a mom?

_____

_____

How much sleep did I get last night?

☐ **More than 8 hours:** I feel like a Disney princess!

☐ **Between 6 and 8 hours:** A few hits on the ol' snooze button, and
I'm good to go.

☐ **Between 3 and 6 hours:** My face is permanently stuck in the yawn
position.

☐ **Between 1 and 3 hours:** I now understand how zombies feel.

☐ **Sleep?** Hahaha! HAHAHAHA!

Extra Mom Notes:

_____

_____

_____

_____

_____

_____

Tuesday

The funniest thing my child did today was:

_____

_____

I ☐ did ☐ didn't laugh because:

_____

_____

What did I do today that made my child laugh?

_____

_____

If I could go back in time, what's one thing that I'd "do over" today?

_____

_____

Today I wished that I was my child's age so that I could

_____

_____!

The mealtime breakdown:

___% Splattered against the wall ___% Eaten by my kid

___% Hidden in the napkin ___% Other: _____

___% Fed to the dog _____

Extra Mom Notes:

_____

_____

_____

_____

_____

_____

What's one thing my child did today that will embarrass him or her when he or she is a teenager?

_____

_____

Today's "Bad Mom" moment:

_____

_____

Today's "Best Mom Ever!" moment:

_____

_____

Based on my child's behavior today, I am sure he or she will grow up to be:

☐ A poet—so quiet and thoughtful!

☐ A boxer—so strong and tough!

☐ A political pundit—so loud and fussy!

☐ An Olympic sprinter—always on the go!

☐ A stand-up comedian—so funny and giggly!

☐ Other: _____ because _____

Extra Mom Notes:

_____

_____

_____

_____

_____

_____

_____

_____

Thursday

What's one lie I told my kid today? (That babies come from storks?
That all of the nutrients are in the bread's crust?)

_____

_____

If a TV camera crew followed me around all day, they'd be filming:

☐ A wacky family sitcom, like *Everybody Loves Raymond* or
Modern Family.

☐ A complex workplace drama, like *Grey's Anatomy* or *The Good Wife.*

☐ A cheesy soap opera, like *Days of Our Lives* or *General Hospital.*

☐ A hyperactive talent contest, like *America's Got Talent* or *So You
Think You Can Dance.*

☐ Other: A _____ show, like

_____

The best actor to play my child would be _____,

because: _____

_____

Based on how I feel today, the best actress to play me would be

_____. She would be perfect because:

_____

_____

Extra Mom Notes:

_____

_____

_____

_____

_____

Friday Favorites!

My child's favorite toy this week was _____

This week, my child's favorite friend was _____

If I had to describe this friend in one word, it would be _____

If I had to describe this friend's parents in one word, it would be

_____

The song my child listened to the most this week was

_____

My feelings about this song:

☐ Love it—one of my favorites!

☐ Like it.

☐ Tolerate it—it could be worse, I guess.

☐ Annoyed by it—it's starting to get on my nerves.

☐ Loathe it—it makes my ears bleed.

The food my child asked for the most this week was _____

I   ☐ did   ☐ didn't   give him or her this food because:

_____

_____

My favorite mom activity is _____ **because:**

_____

_____

Extra Mom Notes:

_____

_____

_____

_____

Saturday

Who was my parenting role model today? (Inspiration can come from anywhere, including your favorite TV character, your own parents, even the patient clerk at your local grocery store!)

_____

_____

If my child remembers one thing about today, I hope he or she remembers this:

_____

_____

Make Your Own Bedtime Story!

Once upon a time there was a _____ kid. That child had a mom who was really _____.

One day, the mom and the kid went on an adventure. First, they went to _____. There they met a big _____, who taught them both how to _____.

"_____!" said the kid. "This is the best _____ ever!"

Next, the mom and the kid went to _____. They played _____ and won!

"That was _____," said the mom, "but now let's go home."

So the mom and the kid went home and ate _____ for dinner. They brushed their teeth, put on their _____, and went to bed.

Extra Mom Notes:

_____

_____

_____

_____

_____

Weekly Look Back

What's one thing that I learned about my child this week?

_____
_____
_____

What's one thing that my child learned about me this week?

_____
_____
_____

What's one thing that I learned about myself?

_____
_____
_____

What's my biggest hope for next week?

_____
_____
_____

Extra Mom Notes:

_____
_____
_____
_____
_____
_____
_____

Monday

What was the cutest thing my child did today?

_____

_____

What did my kid smell like today? (Shampoo? Fruit punch? The family dog?)

_____

_____

What did I do today that I never would have done before I was a mom?

_____

_____

How much sleep did I get last night?

☐ More than 8 hours: I feel like a Disney princess!

☐ Between 6 and 8 hours: A few hits on the ol' snooze button, and I'm good to go.

☐ Between 3 and 6 hours: My face is permanently stuck in the yawn position.

☐ Between 1 and 3 hours: I now understand how zombies feel.

☐ Sleep? Hahaha! HAHAHAHA!

Extra Mom Notes:

_____

_____

_____

_____

_____

_____

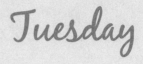

Tuesday

The funniest thing my child did today was:

_____

_____

I ☐ did ☐ didn't laugh because:

_____

_____

What did I do today that made my child laugh?

_____

_____

If I could go back in time, what's one thing that I'd "do over" today?

_____

_____

Today I wished that I was my child's age so that I could

_____

_____!

The mealtime breakdown:

___% Splattered against the wall ___% Eaten by my kid

___% Hidden in the napkin ___% Other: _____

___% Fed to the dog _____

Extra Mom Notes:

_____

_____

_____

_____

_____

Wednesday

What's one thing my child did today that will embarrass him or her when he or she is a teenager?

_____

_____

Today's "Bad Mom" moment:

_____

_____

Today's "Best Mom Ever!" moment:

_____

_____

Based on my child's behavior today, I am sure he or she will grow up to be:

☐ A poet—so quiet and thoughtful!

☐ A boxer—so strong and tough!

☐ A political pundit—so loud and fussy!

☐ An Olympic sprinter—always on the go!

☐ A stand-up comedian—so funny and giggly!

☐ Other: _____ because _____

Extra Mom Notes:

_____

_____

_____

_____

_____

_____

_____

_____

What's one lie I told my kid today? (That babies come from storks? That all of the nutrients are in the bread's crust?)

_____

_____

If a TV camera crew followed me around all day, they'd be filming:

☐ A wacky family sitcom, like *Everybody Loves Raymond* or *Modern Family*.

☐ A complex workplace drama, like *Grey's Anatomy* or *The Good Wife*.

☐ A cheesy soap opera, like *Days of Our Lives* or *General Hospital*.

☐ A hyperactive talent contest, like *America's Got Talent* or *So You Think You Can Dance*.

☐ Other: A _____ show, like

_____

The best actor to play my child would be _____,
because: _____

_____

Based on how I feel today, the best actress to play me would be
_____. She would be perfect because:

_____

_____

Extra Mom Notes:

_____

_____

_____

_____

_____

Friday Favorites! DATE

My child's favorite toy this week was _____

This week, my child's favorite friend was _____

If I had to describe this friend in one word, it would be _____
If I had to describe this friend's parents in one word, it would be
_____

The song my child listened to the most this week was
_____

My feelings about this song:
☐ Love it—one of my favorites!
☐ Like it.
☐ Tolerate it—it could be worse, I guess.
☐ Annoyed by it—it's starting to get on my nerves.
☐ Loathe it—it makes my ears bleed.

The food my child asked for the most this week was _____

I ☐ did ☐ didn't give him or her this food because:
_____
_____

My favorite mom activity is _____ because:
_____
_____

Extra Mom Notes:
_____
_____
_____
_____

Saturday

Who was my parenting role model today? (Inspiration can come from anywhere, including your favorite TV character, your own parents, even the patient clerk at your local grocery store!)

_____

_____

If my child remembers one thing about today, I hope he or she remembers this:

_____

_____

Make Your Own Bedtime Story!

Once upon a time there was a _____ kid. That child had a mom who was really _____.

One day, the mom and the kid went on an adventure. First, they went to _____. There they met a big _____, who taught them both how to _____.

"_____!" said the kid. "This is the best _____ ever!"

Next, the mom and the kid went to _____. They played _____ and won!

"That was _____," said the mom, "but now let's go home."

So the mom and the kid went home and ate _____ for dinner. They brushed their teeth, put on their _____, and went to bed.

Extra Mom Notes:

_____

_____

_____

_____

_____

Sunday

Weekly Look Back

What's one thing that I learned about my child this week?

_____

_____

_____

What's one thing that my child learned about me this week?

_____

_____

_____

What's one thing that I learned about myself?

_____

_____

_____

What's my biggest hope for next week?

_____

_____

_____

Extra Mom Notes:

_____

_____

_____

_____

_____

_____

_____

Monday

What was the cutest thing my child did today?

_____

_____

What did my kid smell like today? (Shampoo? Fruit punch? The family dog?)

_____

_____

What did I do today that I never would have done before I was a mom?

_____

_____

How much sleep did I get last night?

☐ More than 8 hours: I feel like a Disney princess!

☐ Between 6 and 8 hours: A few hits on the ol' snooze button, and I'm good to go.

☐ Between 3 and 6 hours: My face is permanently stuck in the yawn position.

☐ Between 1 and 3 hours: I now understand how zombies feel.

☐ Sleep? Hahaha! HAHAHAHA!

Extra Mom Notes:

_____

_____

_____

_____

_____

_____

_____

Tuesday

The funniest thing my child did today was:

_____

_____

I ☐ did ☐ didn't laugh because:

_____

_____

What did I do today that made my child laugh?

_____

_____

If I could go back in time, what's one thing that I'd "do over" today?

_____

_____

Today I wished that I was my child's age so that I could

_____

_____!

The mealtime breakdown:

___% Splattered against the wall   ___% Eaten by my kid

___% Hidden in the napkin   ___% Other: _____

___% Fed to the dog   _____

Extra Mom Notes:

_____

_____

_____

_____

_____

Wednesday

What's one thing my child did today that will embarrass him or her when he or she is a teenager?

_____

_____

Today's "Bad Mom" moment:

_____

_____

Today's "Best Mom Ever!" moment:

_____

_____

Based on my child's behavior today, I am sure he or she will grow up to be:

☐ A poet—so quiet and thoughtful!

☐ A boxer—so strong and tough!

☐ A political pundit—so loud and fussy!

☐ An Olympic sprinter—always on the go!

☐ A stand-up comedian—so funny and giggly!

☐ Other: _____ because _____

Extra Mom Notes:

_____

_____

_____

_____

_____

_____

_____

_____

Thursday

What's one lie I told my kid today? (That babies come from storks? That all of the nutrients are in the bread's crust?)

_____

_____

If a TV camera crew followed me around all day, they'd be filming:

☐ A wacky family sitcom, like _Everybody Loves Raymond_ or _Modern Family._

☐ A complex workplace drama, like _Grey's Anatomy_ or _The Good Wife._

☐ A cheesy soap opera, like _Days of Our Lives_ or _General Hospital._

☐ A hyperactive talent contest, like _America's Got Talent_ or _So You Think You Can Dance._

☐ Other: A _____ show, like

_____

The best actor to play my child would be _____,

because: _____

_____

Based on how I feel today, the best actress to play me would be

_____. She would be perfect because:

_____

_____

Extra Mom Notes:

_____

_____

_____

_____

_____

Friday Favorites!

My child's favorite toy this week was _____

This week, my child's favorite friend was _____

If I had to describe this friend in one word, it would be _____
If I had to describe this friend's parents in one word, it would be
_____

The song my child listened to the most this week was
_____

My feelings about this song:
☐ Love it—one of my favorites!
☐ Like it.
☐ Tolerate it—it could be worse, I guess.
☐ Annoyed by it—it's starting to get on my nerves.
☐ Loathe it—it makes my ears bleed.

The food my child asked for the most this week was _____

I   ☐ did   ☐ didn't   give him or her this food because:
_____
_____

My favorite mom activity is _____ because:
_____
_____

Extra Mom Notes:
_____
_____
_____
_____

Saturday

Who was my parenting role model today? (Inspiration can come from anywhere, including your favorite TV character, your own parents, even the patient clerk at your local grocery store!)

_____

_____

If my child remembers one thing about today, I hope he or she remembers this:

_____

_____

Make Your Own Bedtime Story!

Once upon a time there was a _____ kid. That child had a mom who was really _____.

One day, the mom and the kid went on an adventure. First, they went to _____. There they met a big _____, who taught them both how to _____.

"_____!" said the kid. "This is the best _____ ever!"

Next, the mom and the kid went to _____. They played _____ and won!

"That was _____," said the mom, "but now let's go home."

So the mom and the kid went home and ate _____ for dinner. They brushed their teeth, put on their _____, and went to bed.

Extra Mom Notes:

_____

_____

_____

_____

_____

Sunday

Weekly Look Back

What's one thing that I learned about my child this week?

_____
_____
_____

What's one thing that my child learned about me this week?

_____
_____
_____

What's one thing that I learned about myself?

_____
_____
_____

What's my biggest hope for next week?

_____
_____
_____

Extra Mom Notes:

_____
_____
_____
_____
_____
_____
_____

Monday

DATE

What was the cutest thing my child did today?

_____

_____

What did my kid smell like today? (Shampoo? Fruit punch? The family dog?)

_____

_____

What did I do today that I never would have done before I was a mom?

_____

_____

How much sleep did I get last night?

☐ **More than 8 hours:** I feel like a Disney princess!

☐ **Between 6 and 8 hours:** A few hits on the ol' snooze button, and I'm good to go.

☐ **Between 3 and 6 hours:** My face is permanently stuck in the yawn position.

☐ **Between 1 and 3 hours:** I now understand how zombies feel.

☐ **Sleep?** Hahaha! HAHAHAHA!

Extra Mom Notes:

_____

_____

_____

_____

_____

_____

Tuesday

The funniest thing my child did today was:

_____

_____

I ☐ did ☐ didn't laugh because:

_____

_____

What did I do today that made my child laugh?

_____

_____

If I could go back in time, what's one thing that I'd "do over" today?

_____

_____

Today I wished that I was my child's age so that I could

_____

_____ !

The mealtime breakdown:

____% Splattered against the wall ____% Eaten by my kid

____% Hidden in the napkin ____% Other: _____

____% Fed to the dog _____

Extra Mom Notes:

_____

_____

_____

_____

_____

Wednesday

What's one thing my child did today that will embarrass him or her when he or she is a teenager?

_____

_____

Today's "Bad Mom" moment:

_____

_____

Today's "Best Mom Ever!" moment:

_____

_____

Based on my child's behavior today, I am sure he or she will grow up to be:

☐ A poet—so quiet and thoughtful!

☐ A boxer—so strong and tough!

☐ A political pundit—so loud and fussy!

☐ An Olympic sprinter—always on the go!

☐ A stand-up comedian—so funny and giggly!

☐ Other: _____ because _____

Extra Mom Notes:

_____

_____

_____

_____

_____

_____

_____

Thursday

What's one lie I told my kid today? (That babies come from storks? That all of the nutrients are in the bread's crust?)

_____

_____

If a TV camera crew followed me around all day, they'd be filming:

☐ A wacky family sitcom, like _Everybody Loves Raymond_ or _Modern Family_.

☐ A complex workplace drama, like _Grey's Anatomy_ or _The Good Wife_.

☐ A cheesy soap opera, like _Days of Our Lives_ or _General Hospital_.

☐ A hyperactive talent contest, like _America's Got Talent_ or _So You Think You Can Dance_.

☐ Other: A _____ show, like

_____

The best actor to play my child would be _____,
because: _____

_____

Based on how I feel today, the best actress to play me would be
_____. She would be perfect because:

_____

_____

Extra Mom Notes:

_____

_____

_____

_____

_____

Friday Favorites! DATE

My child's favorite toy this week was _____

This week, my child's favorite friend was _____

If I had to describe this friend in one word, it would be _____
If I had to describe this friend's parents in one word, it would be

_____

The song my child listened to the most this week was

_____

My feelings about this song:
☐ Love it—one of my favorites!
☐ Like it.
☐ Tolerate it—it could be worse, I guess.
☐ Annoyed by it—it's starting to get on my nerves.
☐ Loathe it—it makes my ears bleed.

The food my child asked for the most this week was _____

I ☐ did ☐ didn't give him or her this food because:

_____

_____

My favorite mom activity is _____ because:

_____

_____

Extra Mom Notes:

_____

_____

_____

_____

Saturday

Who was my parenting role model today? (Inspiration can come from anywhere, including your favorite TV character, your own parents, even the patient clerk at your local grocery store!)

_____

_____

If my child remembers one thing about today, I hope he or she remembers this:

_____

_____

Make Your Own Bedtime Story!

Once upon a time there was a _____ kid. That child had a mom who was really _____.

One day, the mom and the kid went on an adventure. First, they went to _____. There they met a big _____, who taught them both how to _____.

"_____!" said the kid. "This is the best _____ ever!"

Next, the mom and the kid went to _____. They played _____ and won!

"That was _____," said the mom, "but now let's go home."

So the mom and the kid went home and ate _____ for dinner.

They brushed their teeth, put on their _____, and went to bed.

Extra Mom Notes:

_____

_____

_____

_____

_____

Sunday

Weekly Look Back

What's one thing that I learned about my child this week?

_____
_____
_____

What's one thing that my child learned about me this week?

_____
_____
_____

What's one thing that I learned about myself?

_____
_____
_____

What's my biggest hope for next week?

_____
_____
_____

Extra Mom Notes:

_____
_____
_____
_____
_____
_____
_____

What was the cutest thing my child do today?

_____

_____

What did my kid smell like today? (Shampoo? Fruit punch?
The family dog?)

_____

_____

What did I do today that I never would have done before I was
a mom?

_____

_____

How much sleep did I get last night?

☐ More than 8 hours: I feel like a Disney princess!

☐ Between 6 and 8 hours: A few hits on the ol' snooze button, and
I'm good to go.

☐ Between 3 and 6 hours: My face is permanently stuck in the yawn
position.

☐ Between 1 and 3 hours: I now understand how zombies feel.

☐ Sleep? Hahaha! HAHAHAHA!

Extra Mom Notes:

_____

_____

_____

_____

_____

_____

Tuesday

The funniest thing my child did today was:

_____

_____

I ☐ did ☐ didn't laugh because:

_____

_____

What did I do today that made my child laugh?

_____

_____

If I could go back in time, what's one thing that I'd "do over" today?

_____

_____

Today I wished that I was my child's age so that I could

_____

_____!

The mealtime breakdown:

____% Splattered against the wall   ____% Eaten by my kid

____% Hidden in the napkin   ____% Other: _____

____% Fed to the dog

_____

Extra Mom Notes:

_____

_____

_____

_____

_____

_____

Wednesday

What's one thing my child did today that will embarrass him or her when he or she is a teenager?

_____

_____

Today's "Bad Mom" moment:

_____

_____

Today's "Best Mom Ever!" moment:

_____

_____

Based on my child's behavior today, I am sure he or she will grow up to be:

☐ A poet—so quiet and thoughtful!

☐ A boxer—so strong and tough!

☐ A political pundit—so loud and fussy!

☐ An Olympic sprinter—always on the go!

☐ A stand-up comedian—so funny and giggly!

☐ Other: _____ because _____

Extra Mom Notes:

_____

_____

_____

_____

_____

_____

_____

_____

Thursday

What's one lie I told my kid today? (That babies come from storks?
That all of the nutrients are in the bread's crust?)

_____

_____

If a TV camera crew followed me around all day, they'd be filming:

☐ A wacky family sitcom, like _Everybody Loves Raymond_ or
Modern Family.

☐ A complex workplace drama, like _Grey's Anatomy_ or _The Good Wife._

☐ A cheesy soap opera, like _Days of Our Lives_ or _General Hospital._

☐ A hyperactive talent contest, like _America's Got Talent_ or _So You
Think You Can Dance._

☐ Other: A _____ show, like

_____

The best actor to play my child would be _____,
because: _____

_____

Based on how I feel today, the best actress to play me would be
_____. She would be perfect because:

_____

_____

Extra Mom Notes:

_____

_____

_____

_____

_____

Friday Favorites!

My child's favorite toy this week was _____

This week, my child's favorite friend was _____

If I had to describe this friend in one word, it would be _____
If I had to describe this friend's parents in one word, it would be
_____

The song my child listened to the most this week was
_____

My feelings about this song:
☐ Love it—one of my favorites!
☐ Like it.
☐ Tolerate it—it could be worse, I guess.
☐ Annoyed by it—it's starting to get on my nerves.
☐ Loathe it—it makes my ears bleed.

The food my child asked for the most this week was _____

I ☐ did ☐ didn't give him or her this food because:
_____
_____

My favorite mom activity is _____ because:
_____
_____

Extra Mom Notes:
_____
_____
_____
_____

Saturday

Who was my parenting role model today? (Inspiration can come from anywhere, including your favorite TV character, your own parents, even the patient clerk at your local grocery store!)

_____

_____

If my child remembers one thing about today, I hope he or she remembers this:

_____

_____

Make Your Own Bedtime Story!

Once upon a time there was a _____ kid. That child had a mom who was really _____.

One day, the mom and the kid went on an adventure. First, they went to _____. There they met a big _____, who taught them both how to _____.

"_____!" said the kid. "This is the best _____ ever!"

Next, the mom and the kid went to _____. They played _____ and won!

"That was _____," said the mom, "but now let's go home."

So the mom and the kid went home and ate _____ for dinner. They brushed their teeth, put on their _____, and went to bed.

Extra Mom Notes:

_____

_____

_____

_____

_____

Weekly Look Back

What's one thing that I learned about my child this week?

_____
_____
_____

What's one thing that my child learned about me this week?

_____
_____
_____

What's one thing that I learned about myself?

_____
_____
_____

What's my biggest hope for next week?

_____
_____
_____

Extra Mom Notes:

_____
_____
_____
_____
_____
_____
_____

Monday

DATE

What was the cutest thing my child did today?

_____

_____

What did my kid smell like today? (Shampoo? Fruit punch?
The family dog?)

_____

_____

What did I do today that I never would have done before I was
a mom?

_____

_____

How much sleep did I get last night?

☐ More than 8 hours: I feel like a Disney princess!

☐ Between 6 and 8 hours: A few hits on the ol' snooze button, and
I'm good to go.

☐ Between 3 and 6 hours: My face is permanently stuck in the yawn
position.

☐ Between 1 and 3 hours: I now understand how zombies feel.

☐ Sleep? Hahaha! HAHAHAHA!

Extra Mom Notes:

_____

_____

_____

_____

_____

_____

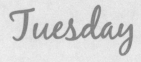

The funniest thing my child did today was:

_____

_____

I ☐ did ☐ didn't laugh because:

_____

_____

What did I do today that made my child laugh?

_____

_____

If I could go back in time, what's one thing that I'd "do over" today?

_____

_____

Today I wished that I was my child's age so that I could

_____

_____!

The mealtime breakdown:

___% Splattered against the wall   ___% Eaten by my kid

___% Hidden in the napkin   ___% Other: _____

___% Fed to the dog   _____

Extra Mom Notes:

_____

_____

_____

_____

_____

Wednesday

What's one thing my child did today that will embarrass him or her when he or she is a teenager?

_____

_____

Today's "Bad Mom" moment:

_____

_____

Today's "Best Mom Ever!" moment:

_____

_____

Based on my child's behavior today, I am sure he or she will grow up to be:

☐ A poet—so quiet and thoughtful!

☐ A boxer—so strong and tough!

☐ A political pundit—so loud and fussy!

☐ An Olympic sprinter—always on the go!

☐ A stand-up comedian—so funny and giggly!

☐ Other: _____ because _____

Extra Mom Notes:

_____

_____

_____

_____

_____

_____

_____

_____

What's one lie I told my kid today? (That babies come from storks? That all of the nutrients are in the bread's crust?)

_____

_____

If a TV camera crew followed me around all day, they'd be filming:

☐ A wacky family sitcom, like *Everybody Loves Raymond* or *Modern Family*.

☐ A complex workplace drama, like *Grey's Anatomy* or *The Good Wife*.

☐ A cheesy soap opera, like *Days of Our Lives* or *General Hospital*.

☐ A hyperactive talent contest, like *America's Got Talent* or *So You Think You Can Dance*.

☐ Other: A _____ show, like

_____

The best actor to play my child would be _____,

because: _____

_____

Based on how I feel today, the best actress to play me would be

_____. She would be perfect because:

_____

_____

Extra Mom Notes:

_____

_____

_____

_____

_____

Friday Favorites! DATE

My child's favorite toy this week was _____

This week, my child's favorite friend was _____

If I had to describe this friend in one word, it would be _____

If I had to describe this friend's parents in one word, it would be

_____

The song my child listened to the most this week was

_____

My feelings about this song:

☐ Love it—one of my favorites!

☐ Like it.

☐ Tolerate it—it could be worse, I guess.

☐ Annoyed by it—it's starting to get on my nerves.

☐ Loathe it—it makes my ears bleed.

The food my child asked for the most this week was _____

I ☐ did ☐ didn't give him or her this food because:

_____

_____

My favorite mom activity is _____ because:

_____

_____

Extra Mom Notes:

_____

_____

_____

_____

Who was my parenting role model today? (Inspiration can come from anywhere, including your favorite TV character, your own parents, even the patient clerk at your local grocery store!)

_____

_____

If my child remembers one thing about today, I hope he or she remembers this:

_____

_____

Make Your Own Bedtime Story!

Once upon a time there was a _____ kid. That child had a mom who was really _____.

One day, the mom and the kid went on an adventure. First, they went to _____. There they met a big _____, who taught them both how to _____.

"_____!" said the kid. "This is the best _____ ever!"

Next, the mom and the kid went to _____. They played _____ and won!

"That was _____," said the mom, "but now let's go home."

So the mom and the kid went home and ate _____ for dinner.

They brushed their teeth, put on their _____, and went to bed.

Extra Mom Notes:

_____

_____

_____

_____

_____

Sunday

Weekly Look Back

What's one thing that I learned about my child this week?

_____
_____
_____

What's one thing that my child learned about me this week?

_____
_____
_____

What's one thing that I learned about myself?

_____
_____
_____

What's my biggest hope for next week?

_____
_____
_____

Extra Mom Notes:

_____
_____
_____
_____
_____
_____
_____

What was the cutest thing my child did today?

_____

_____

What did my kid smell like today? (Shampoo? Fruit punch?
The family dog?)

_____

_____

What did I do today that I never would have done before I was
a mom?

_____

_____

How much sleep did I get last night?

☐ More than 8 hours: I feel like a Disney princess!

☐ Between 6 and 8 hours: A few hits on the ol' snooze button, and
  I'm good to go.

☐ Between 3 and 6 hours: My face is permanently stuck in the yawn
  position.

☐ Between 1 and 3 hours: I now understand how zombies feel.

☐ Sleep? Hahaha! HAHAHAHA!

Extra Mom Notes:

_____

_____

_____

_____

_____

_____

Tuesday

DATE

The funniest thing my child did today was:

_____

_____

I ☐ did ☐ didn't laugh because:

_____

_____

What did I do today that made my child laugh?

_____

_____

If I could go back in time, what's one thing that I'd "do over" today?

_____

_____

Today I wished that I was my child's age so that I could

_____

_____!

The mealtime breakdown:

____% Splattered against the wall   ____% Eaten by my kid

____% Hidden in the napkin   ____% Other: _____

____% Fed to the dog   _____

Extra Mom Notes:

_____

_____

_____

_____

_____

Wednesday

What's one thing my child did today that will embarrass him or her when he or she is a teenager?

_____

_____

Today's "Bad Mom" moment:

_____

_____

Today's "Best Mom Ever!" moment:

_____

_____

Based on my child's behavior today, I am sure he or she will grow up to be:

☐ A poet—so quiet and thoughtful!

☐ A boxer—so strong and tough!

☐ A political pundit—so loud and fussy!

☐ An Olympic sprinter—always on the go!

☐ A stand-up comedian—so funny and giggly!

☐ Other: _____ because _____

Extra Mom Notes:

_____

_____

_____

_____

_____

_____

_____

_____

Thursday

What's one lie I told my kid today? (That babies come from storks?
That all of the nutrients are in the bread's crust?)

_____

_____

If a TV camera crew followed me around all day, they'd be filming:

☐ A wacky family sitcom, like _Everybody Loves Raymond_ or
Modern Family.

☐ A complex workplace drama, like _Grey's Anatomy_ or _The Good Wife._

☐ A cheesy soap opera, like _Days of Our Lives_ or _General Hospital._

☐ A hyperactive talent contest, like _America's Got Talent_ or _So You
Think You Can Dance._

☐ Other: A _____ show, like

_____

The best actor to play my child would be _____,
because: _____

_____

Based on how I feel today, the best actress to play me would be
_____. She would be perfect because:

_____

_____

Extra Mom Notes:

_____

_____

_____

_____

_____

Friday Favorites!

My child's favorite toy this week was _____

This week, my child's favorite friend was _____

If I had to describe this friend in one word, it would be _____
If I had to describe this friend's parents in one word, it would be

_____

The song my child listened to the most this week was

_____

My feelings about this song:
- ☐ Love it—one of my favorites!
- ☐ Like it.
- ☐ Tolerate it—it could be worse, I guess.
- ☐ Annoyed by it—it's starting to get on my nerves.
- ☐ Loathe it—it makes my ears bleed.

The food my child asked for the most this week was _____

I ☐ did ☐ didn't give him or her this food because:

_____

_____

My favorite mom activity is _____ because:

_____

_____

Extra Mom Notes:

_____

_____

_____

_____

Saturday

Who was my parenting role model today? (Inspiration can come from anywhere, including your favorite TV character, your own parents, even the patient clerk at your local grocery store!)

_____

_____

If my child remembers one thing about today, I hope he or she remembers this:

_____

_____

Make Your Own Bedtime Story!

Once upon a time there was a _____ kid. That child had a mom who was really _____.

One day, the mom and the kid went on an adventure. First, they went to _____. There they met a big _____, who taught them both how to _____.

"_____!" said the kid. "This is the best _____ ever!"

Next, the mom and the kid went to _____. They played _____ and won!

"That was _____," said the mom, "but now let's go home."

So the mom and the kid went home and ate _____ for dinner. They brushed their teeth, put on their _____, and went to bed.

Extra Mom Notes:

_____

_____

_____

_____

_____

Sunday

Weekly Look Back

What's one thing that I learned about my child this week?

_____

_____

_____

What's one thing that my child learned about me this week?

_____

_____

_____

What's one thing that I learned about myself?

_____

_____

_____

What's my biggest hope for next week?

_____

_____

_____

Extra Mom Notes:

_____

_____

_____

_____

_____

_____

_____

Monday

What was the cutest thing my child did today?

_____

_____

What did my kid smell like today? (Shampoo? Fruit punch?
The family dog?)

_____

_____

What did I do today that I never would have done before I was
a mom?

_____

_____

How much sleep did I get last night?

☐ More than 8 hours: I feel like a Disney princess!

☐ Between 6 and 8 hours: A few hits on the ol' snooze button, and
I'm good to go.

☐ Between 3 and 6 hours: My face is permanently stuck in the yawn
position.

☐ Between 1 and 3 hours: I now understand how zombies feel.

☐ Sleep? Hahaha! HAHAHAHA!

Extra Mom Notes:

_____

_____

_____

_____

_____

_____

The funniest thing my child did today was:

_____

_____

I ☐ did ☐ didn't laugh because:

_____

_____

What did I do today that made my child laugh?

_____

_____

If I could go back in time, what's one thing that I'd "do over" today?

_____

_____

Today I wished that I was my child's age so that I could

_____

_____ !

The mealtime breakdown:

____% Splattered against the wall   ____% Eaten by my kid

____% Hidden in the napkin   ____% Other: _____

____% Fed to the dog   _____

Extra Mom Notes:

_____

_____

_____

_____

_____

_____

Wednesday

DATE

What's one thing my child did today that will embarrass him or her when he or she is a teenager?

_____

_____

Today's "Bad Mom" moment:

_____

_____

Today's "Best Mom Ever!" moment:

_____

_____

Based on my child's behavior today, I am sure he or she will grow up to be:

☐ A poet—so quiet and thoughtful!

☐ A boxer—so strong and tough!

☐ A political pundit—so loud and fussy!

☐ An Olympic sprinter—always on the go!

☐ A stand-up comedian—so funny and giggly!

☐ Other: _____ because _____

Extra Mom Notes:

_____

_____

_____

_____

_____

_____

_____

Thursday

What's one lie I told my kid today? (That babies come from storks? That all of the nutrients are in the bread's crust?)

_____

_____

If a TV camera crew followed me around all day, they'd be filming:

☐ A wacky family sitcom, like *Everybody Loves Raymond* or *Modern Family*.

☐ A complex workplace drama, like *Grey's Anatomy* or *The Good Wife*.

☐ A cheesy soap opera, like *Days of Our Lives* or *General Hospital*.

☐ A hyperactive talent contest, like *America's Got Talent* or *So You Think You Can Dance*.

☐ Other: A _____ show, like

_____

The best actor to play my child would be _____,

because: _____

_____

Based on how I feel today, the best actress to play me would be

_____. She would be perfect because:

_____

_____

Extra Mom Notes:

_____

_____

_____

_____

_____

Friday Favorites! DATE

My child's favorite toy this week was _____

This week, my child's favorite friend was _____

If I had to describe this friend in one word, it would be _____
If I had to describe this friend's parents in one word, it would be
_____

The song my child listened to the most this week was
_____

My feelings about this song:
- ☐ Love it—one of my favorites!
- ☐ Like it.
- ☐ Tolerate it—it could be worse, I guess.
- ☐ Annoyed by it—it's starting to get on my nerves.
- ☐ Loathe it—it makes my ears bleed.

The food my child asked for the most this week was _____

I ☐ did ☐ didn't give him or her this food because:
_____
_____

My favorite mom activity is _____ because:
_____
_____

Extra Mom Notes:
_____
_____
_____
_____

Who was my parenting role model today? (Inspiration can come from anywhere, including your favorite TV character, your own parents, even the patient clerk at your local grocery store!)

_____

_____

If my child remembers one thing about today, I hope he or she remembers this:

_____

_____

Make Your Own Bedtime Story!

Once upon a time there was a _____ kid. That child had a mom who was really _____.

One day, the mom and the kid went on an adventure. First, they went to _____. There they met a big _____, who taught them both how to _____.

"_____!" said the kid. "This is the best _____ ever!"

Next, the mom and the kid went to _____. They played _____ and won!

"That was _____," said the mom, "but now let's go home."

So the mom and the kid went home and ate _____ for dinner. They brushed their teeth, put on their _____, and went to bed.

Extra Mom Notes:

_____

_____

_____

_____

_____

Sunday

Weekly Look Back

What's one thing that I learned about my child this week?

_____
_____
_____

What's one thing that my child learned about me this week?

_____
_____
_____

What's one thing that I learned about myself?

_____
_____
_____

What's my biggest hope for next week?

_____
_____
_____

Extra Mom Notes:

_____
_____
_____
_____
_____
_____
_____

Monday

What was the cutest thing my child did today?

_____

_____

What did my kid smell like today? (Shampoo? Fruit punch?
The family dog?)

_____

_____

What did I do today that I never would have done before I was
a mom?

_____

_____

How much sleep did I get last night?

☐ **More than 8 hours:** I feel like a Disney princess!

☐ **Between 6 and 8 hours:** A few hits on the ol' snooze button, and
I'm good to go.

☐ **Between 3 and 6 hours:** My face is permanently stuck in the yawn
position.

☐ **Between 1 and 3 hours:** I now understand how zombies feel.

☐ **Sleep?** Hahaha! HAHAHAHA!

Extra Mom Notes:

_____

_____

_____

_____

_____

_____

Tuesday

The funniest thing my child did today was:

_____

_____

I ☐ did ☐ didn't laugh because:

_____

_____

What did I do today that made my child laugh?

_____

_____

If I could go back in time, what's one thing that I'd "do over" today?

_____

_____

Today I wished that I was my child's age so that I could

_____

_____ !

The mealtime breakdown:

___% Splattered against the wall   ___% Eaten by my kid

___% Hidden in the napkin   ___% Other: _____

___% Fed to the dog   _____

Extra Mom Notes:

_____

_____

_____

_____

_____

_____

Wednesday

What's one thing my child did today that will embarrass him or her when he or she is a teenager?

_____

_____

Today's "Bad Mom" moment:

_____

_____

Today's "Best Mom Ever!" moment:

_____

_____

Based on my child's behavior today, I am sure he or she will grow up to be:

☐ A poet—so quiet and thoughtful!

☐ A boxer—so strong and tough!

☐ A political pundit—so loud and fussy!

☐ An Olympic sprinter—always on the go!

☐ A stand-up comedian—so funny and giggly!

☐ Other: _____ because _____

Extra Mom Notes:

_____

_____

_____

_____

_____

_____

_____

_____

Thursday

What's one lie I told my kid today? (That babies come from storks?
That all of the nutrients are in the bread's crust?)

_____

_____

If a TV camera crew followed me around all day, they'd be filming:

☐ A wacky family sitcom, like _Everybody Loves Raymond_ or
   Modern Family.

☐ A complex workplace drama, like _Grey's Anatomy_ or _The Good Wife._

☐ A cheesy soap opera, like _Days of Our Lives_ or _General Hospital._

☐ A hyperactive talent contest, like _America's Got Talent_ or _So You
   Think You Can Dance._

☐ Other: A _____ show, like

_____

The best actor to play my child would be _____,

because: _____

_____

Based on how I feel today, the best actress to play me would be

_____. She would be perfect because:

_____

_____

Extra Mom Notes:

_____

_____

_____

_____

_____

Friday Favorites!

My child's favorite toy this week was _____

This week, my child's favorite friend was _____

If I had to describe this friend in one word, it would be _____

If I had to describe this friend's parents in one word, it would be

_____

The song my child listened to the most this week was

_____

My feelings about this song:

☐ Love it—one of my favorites!

☐ Like it.

☐ Tolerate it—it could be worse, I guess.

☐ Annoyed by it—it's starting to get on my nerves.

☐ Loathe it—it makes my ears bleed.

The food my child asked for the most this week was _____

I   ☐ did   ☐ didn't   give him or her this food because:

_____

_____

My favorite mom activity is _____ because:

_____

_____

Extra Mom Notes:

_____

_____

_____

_____

Saturday

Who was my parenting role model today? (Inspiration can come from anywhere, including your favorite TV character, your own parents, even the patient clerk at your local grocery store!)

_____

_____

If my child remembers one thing about today, I hope he or she remembers this:

_____

_____

Make Your Own Bedtime Story!

Once upon a time there was a _____ kid. That child had a mom who was really _____.

One day, the mom and the kid went on an adventure. First, they went to _____. There they met a big _____, who taught them both how to _____.

"_____!" said the kid. "This is the best _____ ever!"

Next, the mom and the kid went to _____. They played _____ and won!

"That was _____," said the mom, "but now let's go home."

So the mom and the kid went home and ate _____ for dinner. They brushed their teeth, put on their _____, and went to bed.

Extra Mom Notes:

_____

_____

_____

_____

_____

Sunday

Weekly Look Back

What's one thing that I learned about my child this week?

_____
_____
_____

What's one thing that my child learned about me this week?

_____
_____
_____

What's one thing that I learned about myself?

_____
_____
_____

What's my biggest hope for next week?

_____
_____
_____

Extra Mom Notes:

_____
_____
_____
_____
_____
_____
_____

Monday

What was the cutest thing my child did today?

_____
_____

What did my kid smell like today? (Shampoo? Fruit punch?
The family dog?)

_____
_____

What did I do today that I never would have done before I was
a mom?

_____
_____

How much sleep did I get last night?

☐ More than 8 hours: I feel like a Disney princess!

☐ Between 6 and 8 hours: A few hits on the ol' snooze button, and
I'm good to go.

☐ Between 3 and 6 hours: My face is permanently stuck in the yawn
position.

☐ Between 1 and 3 hours: I now understand how zombies feel.

☐ Sleep? Hahaha! HAHAHAHA!

Extra Mom Notes:

_____
_____
_____
_____
_____
_____
_____

Tuesday

The funniest thing my child did today was:

_____

_____

I ☐ did ☐ didn't laugh because:

_____

_____

What did I do today that made my child laugh?

_____

_____

If I could go back in time, what's one thing that I'd "do over" today?

_____

_____

Today I wished that I was my child's age so that I could

_____

_____ !

The mealtime breakdown:

___% Splattered against the wall   ___% Eaten by my kid

___% Hidden in the napkin   ___% Other: _____

___% Fed to the dog   _____

Extra Mom Notes:

_____

_____

_____

_____

_____

Wednesday

What's one thing my child did today that will embarrass him or her when he or she is a teenager?

_____

_____

Today's "Bad Mom" moment:

_____

_____

Today's "Best Mom Ever!" moment:

_____

_____

Based on my child's behavior today, I am sure he or she will grow up to be:

☐ A poet—so quiet and thoughtful!

☐ A boxer—so strong and tough!

☐ A political pundit—so loud and fussy!

☐ An Olympic sprinter—always on the go!

☐ A stand-up comedian—so funny and giggly!

☐ Other: _____ because _____

Extra Mom Notes:

_____

_____

_____

_____

_____

_____

_____

_____

Thursday

What's one lie I told my kid today? (That babies come from storks? That all of the nutrients are in the bread's crust?)

_____

_____

If a TV camera crew followed me around all day, they'd be filming:

☐ A wacky family sitcom, like *Everybody Loves Raymond* or *Modern Family*.

☐ A complex workplace drama, like *Grey's Anatomy* or *The Good Wife*.

☐ A cheesy soap opera, like *Days of Our Lives* or *General Hospital*.

☐ A hyperactive talent contest, like *America's Got Talent* or *So You Think You Can Dance*.

☐ Other: A _____ show, like

_____

The best actor to play my child would be _____,

because: _____

_____

Based on how I feel today, the best actress to play me would be

_____. She would be perfect because:

_____

_____

Extra Mom Notes:

_____

_____

_____

_____

_____

Friday Favorites! DATE

My child's favorite toy this week was _____

This week, my child's favorite friend was _____

If I had to describe this friend in one word, it would be _____
If I had to describe this friend's parents in one word, it would be
_____

The song my child listened to the most this week was
_____

My feelings about this song:
- ☐ Love it—one of my favorites!
- ☐ Like it.
- ☐ Tolerate it—it could be worse, I guess.
- ☐ Annoyed by it—it's starting to get on my nerves.
- ☐ Loathe it—it makes my ears bleed.

The food my child asked for the most this week was _____

I ☐ did ☐ didn't give him or her this food because:
_____
_____

My favorite mom activity is _____ because:
_____
_____

Extra Mom Notes:
_____
_____
_____
_____

Who was my parenting role model today? (Inspiration can come from anywhere, including your favorite TV character, your own parents, even the patient clerk at your local grocery store!)

_____

_____

If my child remembers one thing about today, I hope he or she remembers this:

_____

_____

Make Your Own Bedtime Story!

Once upon a time there was a _____ kid. That child had a mom who was really _____.

One day, the mom and the kid went on an adventure. First, they went to _____. There they met a big _____, who taught them both how to _____.

"_____!" said the kid. "This is the best _____ ever!" Next, the mom and the kid went to _____. They played _____ and won!

"That was _____," said the mom, "but now let's go home." So the mom and the kid went home and ate _____ for dinner. They brushed their teeth, put on their _____, and went to bed.

Extra Mom Notes:

_____

_____

_____

_____

_____

Sunday

Weekly Look Back

What's one thing that I learned about my child this week?

_____
_____
_____

What's one thing that my child learned about me this week?

_____
_____
_____

What's one thing that I learned about myself?

_____
_____
_____

What's my biggest hope for next week?

_____
_____
_____

Extra Mom Notes:

_____
_____
_____
_____
_____
_____
_____
_____

What was the cutest thing my child did today?

_____

_____

What did my kid smell like today? (Shampoo? Fruit punch? The family dog?)

_____

_____

What did I do today that I never would have done before I was a mom?

_____

_____

How much sleep did I get last night?

☐ More than 8 hours: I feel like a Disney princess!

☐ Between 6 and 8 hours: A few hits on the ol' snooze button, and I'm good to go.

☐ Between 3 and 6 hours: My face is permanently stuck in the yawn position.

☐ Between 1 and 3 hours: I now understand how zombies feel.

☐ Sleep? Hahaha! HAHAHAHA!

Extra Mom Notes:

_____

_____

_____

_____

_____

_____

Tuesday

DATE

The funniest thing my child did today was:

_____

_____

I ☐ did ☐ didn't laugh because:

_____

_____

What did I do today that made my child laugh?

_____

_____

If I could go back in time, what's one thing that I'd "do over" today?

_____

_____

Today I wished that I was my child's age so that I could

_____

_____ !

The mealtime breakdown:
___% Splattered against the wall   ___% Eaten by my kid
___% Hidden in the napkin   ___% Other: _____
___% Fed to the dog
_____

Extra Mom Notes:

_____

_____

_____

_____

_____

Wednesday

What's one thing my child did today that will embarrass him or her when he or she is a teenager?

_____

_____

Today's "Bad Mom" moment:

_____

_____

Today's "Best Mom Ever!" moment:

_____

_____

Based on my child's behavior today, I am sure he or she will grow up to be:

☐ A poet—so quiet and thoughtful!

☐ A boxer—so strong and tough!

☐ A political pundit—so loud and fussy!

☐ An Olympic sprinter—always on the go!

☐ A stand-up comedian—so funny and giggly!

☐ Other: _____ because _____

Extra Mom Notes:

_____

_____

_____

_____

_____

_____

_____

_____

Thursday

What's one lie I told my kid today? (That babies come from storks?
That all of the nutrients are in the bread's crust?)

_____

_____

If a TV camera crew followed me around all day, they'd be filming:

☐ A wacky family sitcom, like _Everybody Loves Raymond_ or
   Modern Family.

☐ A complex workplace drama, like _Grey's Anatomy_ or _The Good Wife._

☐ A cheesy soap opera, like _Days of Our Lives_ or _General Hospital._

☐ A hyperactive talent contest, like _America's Got Talent_ or _So You
   Think You Can Dance._

☐ Other: A _____ show, like

_____

The best actor to play my child would be _____,
because: _____

_____

Based on how I feel today, the best actress to play me would be
_____. She would be perfect because:

_____

_____

Extra Mom Notes:

_____

_____

_____

_____

_____

Friday Favorites!

My child's favorite toy this week was _____

This week, my child's favorite friend was _____

If I had to describe this friend in one word, it would be _____
If I had to describe this friend's parents in one word, it would be
_____

The song my child listened to the most this week was
_____

My feelings about this song:
☐ Love it—one of my favorites!
☐ Like it.
☐ Tolerate it—it could be worse, I guess.
☐ Annoyed by it—it's starting to get on my nerves.
☐ Loathe it—it makes my ears bleed.

The food my child asked for the most this week was _____

I ☐ did ☐ didn't give him or her this food because:
_____
_____

My favorite mom activity is _____ **because:**
_____
_____

Extra Mom Notes:
_____
_____
_____
_____

Saturday

Who was my parenting role model today? (Inspiration can come from anywhere, including your favorite TV character, your own parents, even the patient clerk at your local grocery store!)

_____

_____

If my child remembers one thing about today, I hope he or she remembers this:

_____

_____

Make Your Own Bedtime Story!

Once upon a time there was a _____ kid. That child had a mom who was really _____.

One day, the mom and the kid went on an adventure. First, they went to _____. There they met a big _____, who taught them both how to _____.

"_____!" said the kid. "This is the best _____ ever!"

Next, the mom and the kid went to _____. They played _____ and won!

"That was _____," said the mom, "but now let's go home."

So the mom and the kid went home and ate _____ for dinner. They brushed their teeth, put on their _____, and went to bed.

Extra Mom Notes:

_____

_____

_____

_____

_____

Weekly Look Back

What's one thing that I learned about my child this week?

_____
_____
_____

What's one thing that my child learned about me this week?

_____
_____
_____

What's one thing that I learned about myself?

_____
_____
_____

What's my biggest hope for next week?

_____
_____
_____

Extra Mom Notes:

_____
_____
_____
_____
_____
_____
_____

Monday

What was the cutest thing my child did today?

_____
_____

What did my kid smell like today? (Shampoo? Fruit punch? The family dog?)

_____
_____

What did I do today that I never would have done before I was a mom?

_____
_____

How much sleep did I get last night?

☐ More than 8 hours: I feel like a Disney princess!
☐ Between 6 and 8 hours: A few hits on the ol' snooze button, and I'm good to go.
☐ Between 3 and 6 hours: My face is permanently stuck in the yawn position.
☐ Between 1 and 3 hours: I now understand how zombies feel.
☐ Sleep? Hahaha! HAHAHAHA!

Extra Mom Notes:

_____
_____
_____
_____
_____
_____
_____

Tuesday

The funniest thing my child did today was:

_____

_____

I ☐ did ☐ didn't laugh because:

_____

_____

What did I do today that made my child laugh?

_____

_____

If I could go back in time, what's one thing that I'd "do over" today?

_____

_____

Today I wished that I was my child's age so that I could

_____

_____!

The mealtime breakdown:

___% Splattered against the wall   ___% Eaten by my kid

___% Hidden in the napkin   ___% Other: _____

___% Fed to the dog   _____

Extra Mom Notes:

_____

_____

_____

_____

_____

Wednesday

What's one thing my child did today that will embarrass him or her when he or she is a teenager?

_____

_____

Today's "Bad Mom" moment:

_____

_____

Today's "Best Mom Ever!" moment:

_____

_____

Based on my child's behavior today, I am sure he or she will grow up to be:

☐ A poet—so quiet and thoughtful!

☐ A boxer—so strong and tough!

☐ A political pundit—so loud and fussy!

☐ An Olympic sprinter—always on the go!

☐ A stand-up comedian—so funny and giggly!

☐ Other: _____ because _____

Extra Mom Notes:

_____

_____

_____

_____

_____

_____

_____

_____

Thursday

What's one lie I told my kid today? (That babies come from storks?
That all of the nutrients are in the bread's crust?)

_____

_____

If a TV camera crew followed me around all day, they'd be filming:

☐ A wacky family sitcom, like _Everybody Loves Raymond_ or
Modern Family.

☐ A complex workplace drama, like _Grey's Anatomy_ or _The Good Wife._

☐ A cheesy soap opera, like _Days of Our Lives_ or _General Hospital._

☐ A hyperactive talent contest, like _America's Got Talent_ or _So You
Think You Can Dance._

☐ Other: A _____ show, like

_____

The best actor to play my child would be _____,
because: _____

_____

Based on how I feel today, the best actress to play me would be
_____. She would be perfect because:

_____

_____

Extra Mom Notes:

_____

_____

_____

_____

_____

Friday Favorites! DATE _____

My child's favorite toy this week was _____

This week, my child's favorite friend was _____

If I had to describe this friend in one word, it would be _____
If I had to describe this friend's parents in one word, it would be
_____

The song my child listened to the most this week was
_____

My feelings about this song:
- ☐ Love it—one of my favorites!
- ☐ Like it.
- ☐ Tolerate it—it could be worse, I guess.
- ☐ Annoyed by it—it's starting to get on my nerves.
- ☐ Loathe it—it makes my ears bleed.

The food my child asked for the most this week was _____

I ☐ did ☐ didn't give him or her this food because:
_____
_____

My favorite mom activity is _____ because:
_____
_____

Extra Mom Notes:
_____
_____
_____
_____

Who was my parenting role model today? (Inspiration can come from anywhere, including your favorite TV character, your own parents, even the patient clerk at your local grocery store!)

_____

_____

If my child remembers one thing about today, I hope he or she remembers this:

_____

_____

Make Your Own Bedtime Story!

Once upon a time there was a _____ kid. That child had a mom who was really _____.

One day, the mom and the kid went on an adventure. First, they went to _____. There they met a big _____, who taught them both how to _____.

"_____!" said the kid. "This is the best _____ ever!"

Next, the mom and the kid went to _____. They played _____ and won!

"That was _____," said the mom, "but now let's go home."

So the mom and the kid went home and ate _____ for dinner. They brushed their teeth, put on their _____, and went to bed.

Extra Mom Notes:

_____

_____

_____

_____

_____

Sunday

Weekly Look Back

What's one thing that I learned about my child this week?

_____
_____
_____

What's one thing that my child learned about me this week?

_____
_____
_____

What's one thing that I learned about myself?

_____
_____
_____

What's my biggest hope for next week?

_____
_____
_____

Extra Mom Notes:

_____
_____
_____
_____
_____
_____
_____
_____

What was the cutest thing my child did today?

_____

_____

What did my kid smell like today? (Shampoo? Fruit punch? The family dog?)

_____

_____

What did I do today that I never would have done before I was a mom?

_____

_____

How much sleep did I get last night?

☐ More than 8 hours: I feel like a Disney princess!

☐ Between 6 and 8 hours: A few hits on the ol' snooze button, and I'm good to go.

☐ Between 3 and 6 hours: My face is permanently stuck in the yawn position.

☐ Between 1 and 3 hours: I now understand how zombies feel.

☐ Sleep? Hahaha! HAHAHAHA!

Extra Mom Notes:

_____

_____

_____

_____

_____

_____

_____

Tuesday

The funniest thing my child did today was:

_____

_____

I ☐ did ☐ didn't laugh because:

_____

_____

What did I do today that made my child laugh?

_____

_____

If I could go back in time, what's one thing that I'd "do over" today?

_____

_____

Today I wished that I was my child's age so that I could

_____

_____!

The mealtime breakdown:

___% Splattered against the wall ___% Eaten by my kid

___% Hidden in the napkin ___% Other: _____

___% Fed to the dog _____

Extra Mom Notes:

_____

_____

_____

_____

_____

Wednesday

What's one thing my child did today that will embarrass him or her when he or she is a teenager?

_____
_____

Today's "Bad Mom" moment:

_____
_____

Today's "Best Mom Ever!" moment:

_____
_____

Based on my child's behavior today, I am sure he or she will grow up to be:

☐ A poet—so quiet and thoughtful!
☐ A boxer—so strong and tough!
☐ A political pundit—so loud and fussy!
☐ An Olympic sprinter—always on the go!
☐ A stand-up comedian—so funny and giggly!
☐ Other: _____ because _____

Extra Mom Notes:

_____
_____
_____
_____
_____
_____
_____
_____

Thursday

What's one lie I told my kid today? (That babies come from storks?
That all of the nutrients are in the bread's crust?)

_____

_____

If a TV camera crew followed me around all day, they'd be filming:

☐ A wacky family sitcom, like _Everybody Loves Raymond_ or
  Modern Family.

☐ A complex workplace drama, like _Grey's Anatomy_ or _The Good Wife._

☐ A cheesy soap opera, like _Days of Our Lives_ or _General Hospital._

☐ A hyperactive talent contest, like _America's Got Talent_ or _So You
  Think You Can Dance._

☐ Other: A _____ show, like

_____

The best actor to play my child would be _____,

because: _____

_____

Based on how I feel today, the best actress to play me would be

_____. She would be perfect because:

_____

_____

Extra Mom Notes:

_____

_____

_____

_____

_____

Friday Favorites!

My child's favorite toy this week was _____

This week, my child's favorite friend was _____

If I had to describe this friend in one word, it would be _____
If I had to describe this friend's parents in one word, it would be

_____

The song my child listened to the most this week was

_____

My feelings about this song:
- ☐ Love it—one of my favorites!
- ☐ Like it.
- ☐ Tolerate it—it could be worse, I guess.
- ☐ Annoyed by it—it's starting to get on my nerves.
- ☐ Loathe it—it makes my ears bleed.

The food my child asked for the most this week was _____

I ☐ did ☐ didn't give him or her this food because:

_____

_____

My favorite mom activity is _____ because:

_____

_____

Extra Mom Notes:

_____

_____

_____

_____

Saturday

Who was my parenting role model today? (Inspiration can come from anywhere, including your favorite TV character, your own parents, even the patient clerk at your local grocery store!)

_____

_____

If my child remembers one thing about today, I hope he or she remembers this:

_____

_____

Make Your Own Bedtime Story!

Once upon a time there was a _____ kid. That child had a mom who was really _____.

One day, the mom and the kid went on an adventure. First, they went to _____. There they met a big _____, who taught them both how to _____.

"_____!" said the kid. "This is the best _____ ever!"

Next, the mom and the kid went to _____. They played _____ and won!

"That was _____," said the mom, "but now let's go home."

So the mom and the kid went home and ate _____ for dinner. They brushed their teeth, put on their _____, and went to bed.

Extra Mom Notes:

_____

_____

_____

_____

_____

Sunday

Weekly Look Back

What's one thing that I learned about my child this week?

_____
_____
_____

What's one thing that my child learned about me this week?

_____
_____
_____

What's one thing that I learned about myself?

_____
_____
_____

What's my biggest hope for next week?

_____
_____
_____

Extra Mom Notes:

_____
_____
_____
_____
_____
_____
_____

Monday

What was the cutest thing my child did today?

_____

_____

What did my kid smell like today? (Shampoo? Fruit punch? The family dog?)

_____

_____

What did I do today that I never would have done before I was a mom?

_____

_____

How much sleep did I get last night?

☐ **More than 8 hours:** I feel like a Disney princess!

☐ **Between 6 and 8 hours:** A few hits on the ol' snooze button, and I'm good to go.

☐ **Between 3 and 6 hours:** My face is permanently stuck in the yawn position.

☐ **Between 1 and 3 hours:** I now understand how zombies feel.

☐ **Sleep?** Hahaha! HAHAHAHA!

Extra Mom Notes:

_____

_____

_____

_____

_____

_____

The funniest thing my child did today was:

_____

_____

I ☐ did ☐ didn't laugh because:

_____

_____

What did I do today that made my child laugh?

_____

_____

If I could go back in time, what's one thing that I'd "do over" today?

_____

_____

Today I wished that I was my child's age so that I could

_____

_____!

The mealtime breakdown:

___% Splattered against the wall   ___% Eaten by my kid

___% Hidden in the napkin   ___% Other: _____

___% Fed to the dog   _____

Extra Mom Notes:

_____

_____

_____

_____

_____

Wednesday

What's one thing my child did today that will embarrass him or her when he or she is a teenager?

_____

_____

Today's "Bad Mom" moment:

_____

_____

Today's "Best Mom Ever!" moment:

_____

_____

Based on my child's behavior today, I am sure he or she will grow up to be:

☐ A poet—so quiet and thoughtful!

☐ A boxer—so strong and tough!

☐ A political pundit—so loud and fussy!

☐ An Olympic sprinter—always on the go!

☐ A stand-up comedian—so funny and giggly!

☐ Other: _____ because _____

Extra Mom Notes:

_____

_____

_____

_____

_____

_____

_____

_____

Thursday

What's one lie I told my kid today? (That babies come from storks? That all of the nutrients are in the bread's crust?)

_____

_____

If a TV camera crew followed me around all day, they'd be filming:

☐ A wacky family sitcom, like _Everybody Loves Raymond_ or _Modern Family._

☐ A complex workplace drama, like _Grey's Anatomy_ or _The Good Wife._

☐ A cheesy soap opera, like _Days of Our Lives_ or _General Hospital._

☐ A hyperactive talent contest, like _America's Got Talent_ or _So You Think You Can Dance._

☐ Other: A _____ show, like

_____

The best actor to play my child would be _____,
because: _____

_____

Based on how I feel today, the best actress to play me would be
_____. She would be perfect because:

_____

_____

Extra Mom Notes:

_____

_____

_____

_____

_____

Friday Favorites! DATE

My child's favorite toy this week was _____

This week, my child's favorite friend was _____

If I had to describe this friend in one word, it would be _____
If I had to describe this friend's parents in one word, it would be
_____

The song my child listened to the most this week was
_____

My feelings about this song:
- ☐ Love it—one of my favorites!
- ☐ Like it.
- ☐ Tolerate it—it could be worse, I guess.
- ☐ Annoyed by it—it's starting to get on my nerves.
- ☐ Loathe it—it makes my ears bleed.

The food my child asked for the most this week was _____

I ☐ did ☐ didn't give him or her this food because:
_____
_____

My favorite mom activity is _____ because:
_____
_____

Extra Mom Notes:
_____
_____
_____
_____

Who was my parenting role model today? (Inspiration can come from anywhere, including your favorite TV character, your own parents, even the patient clerk at your local grocery store!)

_____

_____

If my child remembers one thing about today, I hope he or she remembers this:

_____

_____

Make Your Own Bedtime Story!

Once upon a time there was a _____ kid. That child had a mom who was really _____.

One day, the mom and the kid went on an adventure. First, they went to _____. There they met a big _____, who taught them both how to _____.

"_____!" said the kid. "This is the best _____ ever!"

Next, the mom and the kid went to _____. They played _____ and won!

"That was _____," said the mom, "but now let's go home."

So the mom and the kid went home and ate _____ for dinner. They brushed their teeth, put on their _____, and went to bed.

Extra Mom Notes:

_____

_____

_____

_____

_____

Sunday

DATE

Weekly Look Back

What's one thing that I learned about my child this week?

_____
_____
_____

What's one thing that my child learned about me this week?

_____
_____
_____

What's one thing that I learned about myself?

_____
_____
_____

What's my biggest hope for next week?

_____
_____
_____

Extra Mom Notes:

_____
_____
_____
_____
_____
_____
_____

Monday

What was the cutest thing my child did today?

_____

_____

What did my kid smell like today? (Shampoo? Fruit punch? The family dog?)

_____

_____

What did I do today that I never would have done before I was a mom?

_____

_____

How much sleep did I get last night?

☐ **More than 8 hours:** I feel like a Disney princess!

☐ **Between 6 and 8 hours:** A few hits on the ol' snooze button, and I'm good to go.

☐ **Between 3 and 6 hours:** My face is permanently stuck in the yawn position.

☐ **Between 1 and 3 hours:** I now understand how zombies feel.

☐ **Sleep?** Hahaha! HAHAHAHA!

Extra Mom Notes:

_____

_____

_____

_____

_____

_____

Tuesday

DATE

The funniest thing my child did today was:

_____

_____

I ☐ did ☐ didn't **laugh because:**

_____

_____

What did I do today that made my child laugh?

_____

_____

If I could go back in time, what's one thing that I'd "do over" today?

_____

_____

Today I wished that I was my child's age so that I could

_____

_____!

The mealtime breakdown:

___% Splattered against the wall   ___% Eaten by my kid

___% Hidden in the napkin   ___% Other: _____

___% Fed to the dog   _____

Extra Mom Notes:

_____

_____

_____

_____

_____

Wednesday

What's one thing my child did today that will embarrass him or her when he or she is a teenager?

_____

_____

Today's "Bad Mom" moment:

_____

_____

Today's "Best Mom Ever!" moment:

_____

_____

Based on my child's behavior today, I am sure he or she will grow up to be:

☐ A poet—so quiet and thoughtful!

☐ A boxer—so strong and tough!

☐ A political pundit—so loud and fussy!

☐ An Olympic sprinter—always on the go!

☐ A stand-up comedian—so funny and giggly!

☐ Other: _____ because _____

Extra Mom Notes:

_____

_____

_____

_____

_____

_____

_____

_____

Thursday

What's one lie I told my kid today? (That babies come from storks? That all of the nutrients are in the bread's crust?)

_____

_____

If a TV camera crew followed me around all day, they'd be filming:

☐ A wacky family sitcom, like _Everybody Loves Raymond_ or _Modern Family._

☐ A complex workplace drama, like _Grey's Anatomy_ or _The Good Wife._

☐ A cheesy soap opera, like _Days of Our Lives_ or _General Hospital._

☐ A hyperactive talent contest, like _America's Got Talent_ or _So You Think You Can Dance._

☐ Other: A _____ show, like

_____

The best actor to play my child would be _____,

because: _____

_____

Based on how I feel today, the best actress to play me would be

_____. She would be perfect because:

_____

_____

Extra Mom Notes:

_____

_____

_____

_____

_____

Friday Favorites!

My child's favorite toy this week was _____

This week, my child's favorite friend was _____

If I had to describe this friend in one word, it would be _____

If I had to describe this friend's parents in one word, it would be

_____

The song my child listened to the most this week was

_____

My feelings about this song:

☐ Love it—one of my favorites!

☐ Like it.

☐ Tolerate it—it could be worse, I guess.

☐ Annoyed by it—it's starting to get on my nerves.

☐ Loathe it—it makes my ears bleed.

The food my child asked for the most this week was _____

I ☐ did ☐ didn't give him or her this food because:

_____

_____

My favorite mom activity is _____ because:

_____

_____

Extra Mom Notes:

_____

_____

_____

_____

Saturday

Who was my parenting role model today? (Inspiration can come from anywhere, including your favorite TV character, your own parents, even the patient clerk at your local grocery store!)

_____

_____

If my child remembers one thing about today, I hope he or she remembers this:

_____

_____

Make Your Own Bedtime Story!

Once upon a time there was a _____ kid. That child had a mom who was really _____.

One day, the mom and the kid went on an adventure. First, they went to _____. There they met a big _____, who taught them both how to _____.

"_____!" said the kid. "This is the best _____ ever!"

Next, the mom and the kid went to _____. They played _____ and won!

"That was _____," said the mom, "but now let's go home."

So the mom and the kid went home and ate _____ for dinner.

They brushed their teeth, put on their _____, and went to bed.

Extra Mom Notes:

_____

_____

_____

_____

_____

Weekly Look Back

What's one thing that I learned about my child this week?

_____

_____

_____

What's one thing that my child learned about me this week?

_____

_____

_____

What's one thing that I learned about myself?

_____

_____

_____

What's my biggest hope for next week?

_____

_____

_____

Extra Mom Notes:

_____

_____

_____

_____

_____

_____

_____

Monday

What was the cutest thing my child did today?

_____

_____

What did my kid smell like today? (Shampoo? Fruit punch? The family dog?)

_____

_____

What did I do today that I never would have done before I was a mom?

_____

_____

How much sleep did I get last night?

☐ **More than 8 hours:** I feel like a Disney princess!

☐ **Between 6 and 8 hours:** A few hits on the ol' snooze button, and I'm good to go.

☐ **Between 3 and 6 hours:** My face is permanently stuck in the yawn position.

☐ **Between 1 and 3 hours:** I now understand how zombies feel.

☐ **Sleep?** Hahaha! HAHAHAHA!

Extra Mom Notes:

_____

_____

_____

_____

_____

_____

The funniest thing my child did today was:

_____

_____

I ☐ did ☐ didn't laugh because:

_____

_____

What did I do today that made my child laugh?

_____

_____

If I could go back in time, what's one thing that I'd "do over" today?

_____

_____

Today I wished that I was my child's age so that I could

_____

_____ !

The mealtime breakdown:

____% Splattered against the wall   ____% Eaten by my kid

____% Hidden in the napkin   ____% Other: _____

____% Fed to the dog   _____

Extra Mom Notes:

_____

_____

_____

_____

_____

Wednesday

What's one thing my child did today that will embarrass him or her when he or she is a teenager?

_____

_____

Today's "Bad Mom" moment:

_____

_____

Today's "Best Mom Ever!" moment:

_____

_____

Based on my child's behavior today, I am sure he or she will grow up to be:

☐ A poet—so quiet and thoughtful!

☐ A boxer—so strong and tough!

☐ A political pundit—so loud and fussy!

☐ An Olympic sprinter—always on the go!

☐ A stand-up comedian—so funny and giggly!

☐ Other: _____ because _____

Extra Mom Notes:

_____

_____

_____

_____

_____

_____

_____

_____

Thursday

What's one lie I told my kid today? (That babies come from storks? That all of the nutrients are in the bread's crust?)

_____

_____

If a TV camera crew followed me around all day, they'd be filming:

☐ A wacky family sitcom, like *Everybody Loves Raymond* or *Modern Family*.

☐ A complex workplace drama, like *Grey's Anatomy* or *The Good Wife*.

☐ A cheesy soap opera, like *Days of Our Lives* or *General Hospital*.

☐ A hyperactive talent contest, like *America's Got Talent* or *So You Think You Can Dance*.

☐ Other: A _____ show, like

_____

The best actor to play my child would be _____,

because: _____

_____

Based on how I feel today, the best actress to play me would be

_____. She would be perfect because:

_____

_____

Extra Mom Notes:

_____

_____

_____

_____

_____

Friday Favorites! DATE

My child's favorite toy this week was _____

This week, my child's favorite friend was _____

If I had to describe this friend in one word, it would be _____
If I had to describe this friend's parents in one word, it would be
_____

The song my child listened to the most this week was
_____

My feelings about this song:
☐ Love it—one of my favorites!
☐ Like it.
☐ Tolerate it—it could be worse, I guess.
☐ Annoyed by it—it's starting to get on my nerves.
☐ Loathe it—it makes my ears bleed.

The food my child asked for the most this week was _____

I   ☐ did   ☐ didn't   give him or her this food because:
_____
_____

My favorite mom activity is _____ because:
_____
_____

Extra Mom Notes:
_____
_____
_____
_____

Who was my parenting role model today? (Inspiration can come from anywhere, including your favorite TV character, your own parents, even the patient clerk at your local grocery store!)

_____

_____

If my child remembers one thing about today, I hope he or she remembers this:

_____

_____

Make Your Own Bedtime Story!

Once upon a time there was a _____ kid. That child had a mom who was really _____.

One day, the mom and the kid went on an adventure. First, they went to _____. There they met a big _____, who taught them both how to _____.

"_____!" said the kid. "This is the best _____ ever!"

Next, the mom and the kid went to _____. They played _____ and won!

"That was _____," said the mom, "but now let's go home."

So the mom and the kid went home and ate _____ for dinner. They brushed their teeth, put on their _____, and went to bed.

Extra Mom Notes:

_____

_____

_____

_____

_____

Sunday

Weekly Look Back

What's one thing that I learned about my child this week?

_____
_____
_____

What's one thing that my child learned about me this week?

_____
_____
_____

What's one thing that I learned about myself?

_____
_____
_____

What's my biggest hope for next week?

_____
_____
_____

Extra Mom Notes:

_____
_____
_____
_____
_____
_____
_____

Monday

What was the cutest thing my child did today?

_____

_____

What did my kid smell like today? (Shampoo? Fruit punch? The family dog?)

_____

_____

What did I do today that I never would have done before I was a mom?

_____

_____

How much sleep did I get last night?

☐ More than 8 hours: I feel like a Disney princess!

☐ Between 6 and 8 hours: A few hits on the ol' snooze button, and I'm good to go.

☐ Between 3 and 6 hours: My face is permanently stuck in the yawn position.

☐ Between 1 and 3 hours: I now understand how zombies feel.

☐ Sleep? Hahaha! HAHAHAHA!

Extra Mom Notes:

_____

_____

_____

_____

_____

_____

Tuesday

The funniest thing my child did today was:

_____

_____

I ☐ did ☐ didn't laugh because:

_____

_____

What did I do today that made my child laugh?

_____

_____

If I could go back in time, what's one thing that I'd "do over" today?

_____

_____

Today I wished that I was my child's age so that I could

_____

_____!

The mealtime breakdown:

___% Splattered against the wall   ___% Eaten by my kid

___% Hidden in the napkin   ___% Other: _____

___% Fed to the dog   _____

Extra Mom Notes:

_____

_____

_____

_____

_____

Wednesday

What's one thing my child did today that will embarrass him or her when he or she is a teenager?

_____

_____

Today's "Bad Mom" moment:

_____

_____

Today's "Best Mom Ever!" moment:

_____

_____

Based on my child's behavior today, I am sure he or she will grow up to be:

☐ A poet—so quiet and thoughtful!

☐ A boxer—so strong and tough!

☐ A political pundit—so loud and fussy!

☐ An Olympic sprinter—always on the go!

☐ A stand-up comedian—so funny and giggly!

☐ Other: _____ because _____

Extra Mom Notes:

_____

_____

_____

_____

_____

_____

_____

_____

Thursday

What's one lie I told my kid today? (That babies come from storks?
That all of the nutrients are in the bread's crust?)

_____

_____

If a TV camera crew followed me around all day, they'd be filming:

☐ A wacky family sitcom, like _Everybody Loves Raymond_ or
   Modern Family.

☐ A complex workplace drama, like _Grey's Anatomy_ or _The Good Wife._

☐ A cheesy soap opera, like _Days of Our Lives_ or _General Hospital._

☐ A hyperactive talent contest, like _America's Got Talent_ or _So You
   Think You Can Dance._

☐ Other: A _____ show, like

_____

The best actor to play my child would be _____,
because: _____

_____

Based on how I feel today, the best actress to play me would be
_____. She would be perfect because:

_____

_____

Extra Mom Notes:

_____

_____

_____

_____

_____

Friday Favorites!

My child's favorite toy this week was _____

This week, my child's favorite friend was _____

If I had to describe this friend in one word, it would be _____
If I had to describe this friend's parents in one word, it would be
_____

The song my child listened to the most this week was
_____

My feelings about this song:
- ☐ Love it—one of my favorites!
- ☐ Like it.
- ☐ Tolerate it—it could be worse, I guess.
- ☐ Annoyed by it—it's starting to get on my nerves.
- ☐ Loathe it—it makes my ears bleed.

The food my child asked for the most this week was _____

I ☐ did   ☐ didn't   give him or her this food because:
_____
_____

My favorite mom activity is _____ because:
_____
_____

Extra Mom Notes:
_____
_____
_____
_____

Saturday

Who was my parenting role model today? (Inspiration can come from anywhere, including your favorite TV character, your own parents, even the patient clerk at your local grocery store!)

_____

_____

If my child remembers one thing about today, I hope he or she remembers this:

_____

_____

Make Your Own Bedtime Story!

Once upon a time there was a _____ kid. That child had a mom who was really _____.

One day, the mom and the kid went on an adventure. First, they went to _____. There they met a big _____, who taught them both how to _____.

"_____!" said the kid. "This is the best _____ ever!"

Next, the mom and the kid went to _____. They played _____ and won!

"That was _____," said the mom, "but now let's go home."

So the mom and the kid went home and ate _____ for dinner.

They brushed their teeth, put on their _____, and went to bed.

Extra Mom Notes:

_____

_____

_____

_____

_____

Sunday

Weekly Look Back

What's one thing that I learned about my child this week?

_____
_____
_____

What's one thing that my child learned about me this week?

_____
_____
_____

What's one thing that I learned about myself?

_____
_____
_____

What's my biggest hope for next week?

_____
_____
_____

Extra Mom Notes:

_____
_____
_____
_____
_____
_____
_____

Monday

What was the cutest thing my child did today?

_____

_____

What did my kid smell like today? (Shampoo? Fruit punch? The family dog?)

_____

_____

What did I do today that I never would have done before I was a mom?

_____

_____

How much sleep did I get last night?

☐ More than 8 hours: I feel like a Disney princess!

☐ Between 6 and 8 hours: A few hits on the ol' snooze button, and I'm good to go.

☐ Between 3 and 6 hours: My face is permanently stuck in the yawn position.

☐ Between 1 and 3 hours: I now understand how zombies feel.

☐ Sleep? Hahaha! HAHAHAHA!

Extra Mom Notes:

_____

_____

_____

_____

_____

_____

_____

Tuesday

The funniest thing my child did today was:

_____

_____

I ☐ did ☐ didn't laugh because:

_____

_____

What did I do today that made my child laugh?

_____

_____

If I could go back in time, what's one thing that I'd "do over" today?

_____

_____

Today I wished that I was my child's age so that I could

_____

_____!

The mealtime breakdown:

____% Splattered against the wall   ____% Eaten by my kid

____% Hidden in the napkin   ____% Other: _____

____% Fed to the dog   _____

Extra Mom Notes:

_____

_____

_____

_____

_____

_____

Wednesday

What's one thing my child did today that will embarrass him or her when he or she is a teenager?

_____

_____

Today's "Bad Mom" moment:

_____

_____

Today's "Best Mom Ever!" moment:

_____

_____

Based on my child's behavior today, I am sure he or she will grow up to be:

☐ A poet—so quiet and thoughtful!

☐ A boxer—so strong and tough!

☐ A political pundit—so loud and fussy!

☐ An Olympic sprinter—always on the go!

☐ A stand-up comedian—so funny and giggly!

☐ Other: _____ because _____

Extra Mom Notes:

_____

_____

_____

_____

_____

_____

_____

_____

Thursday

What's one lie I told my kid today? (That babies come from storks? That all of the nutrients are in the bread's crust?)

_____

_____

If a TV camera crew followed me around all day, they'd be filming:

☐ A wacky family sitcom, like *Everybody Loves Raymond* or *Modern Family.*

☐ A complex workplace drama, like *Grey's Anatomy* or *The Good Wife.*

☐ A cheesy soap opera, like *Days of Our Lives* or *General Hospital.*

☐ A hyperactive talent contest, like *America's Got Talent* or *So You Think You Can Dance.*

☐ Other: A _____ show, like

_____

The best actor to play my child would be _____,

because: _____

_____

Based on how I feel today, the best actress to play me would be

_____. She would be perfect because:

_____

_____

Extra Mom Notes:

_____

_____

_____

_____

_____

Friday Favorites! DATE _____

My child's favorite toy this week was _____

This week, my child's favorite friend was _____

If I had to describe this friend in one word, it would be _____
If I had to describe this friend's parents in one word, it would be
_____

The song my child listened to the most this week was
_____

My feelings about this song:
☐ Love it—one of my favorites!
☐ Like it.
☐ Tolerate it—it could be worse, I guess.
☐ Annoyed by it—it's starting to get on my nerves.
☐ Loathe it—it makes my ears bleed.

The food my child asked for the most this week was _____

I ☐ did ☐ didn't give him or her this food because:
_____
_____

My favorite mom activity is _____ because:
_____
_____

Extra Mom Notes:
_____
_____
_____
_____

Who was my parenting role model today? (Inspiration can come from anywhere, including your favorite TV character, your own parents, even the patient clerk at your local grocery store!)

_____

_____

If my child remembers one thing about today, I hope he or she remembers this:

_____

_____

Make Your Own Bedtime Story!

Once upon a time there was a _____ kid. That child had a mom who was really _____.

One day, the mom and the kid went on an adventure. First, they went to _____. There they met a big _____, who taught them both how to _____.

"_____!" said the kid. "This is the best _____ ever!"

Next, the mom and the kid went to _____. They played _____ and won!

"That was _____," said the mom, "but now let's go home."

So the mom and the kid went home and ate _____ for dinner. They brushed their teeth, put on their _____, and went to bed.

Extra Mom Notes:

_____

_____

_____

_____

_____

Sunday

Weekly Look Back

What's one thing that I learned about my child this week?

_____
_____
_____

What's one thing that my child learned about me this week?

_____
_____
_____

What's one thing that I learned about myself?

_____
_____
_____

What's my biggest hope for next week?

_____
_____
_____

Extra Mom Notes:

_____
_____
_____
_____
_____
_____
_____

Monday

What was the cutest thing my child did today?

_____

_____

What did my kid smell like today? (Shampoo? Fruit punch? The family dog?)

_____

_____

What did I do today that I never would have done before I was a mom?

_____

_____

How much sleep did I get last night?

☐ **More than 8 hours:** I feel like a Disney princess!

☐ **Between 6 and 8 hours:** A few hits on the ol' snooze button, and I'm good to go.

☐ **Between 3 and 6 hours:** My face is permanently stuck in the yawn position.

☐ **Between 1 and 3 hours:** I now understand how zombies feel.

☐ **Sleep?** Hahaha! HAHAHAHA!

Extra Mom Notes:

_____

_____

_____

_____

_____

_____

_____

Tuesday

The funniest thing my child did today was:

_____

_____

I ☐ did ☐ didn't   laugh because:

_____

_____

What did I do today that made my child laugh?

_____

_____

If I could go back in time, what's one thing that I'd "do over" today?

_____

_____

Today I wished that I was my child's age so that I could

_____

_____!

The mealtime breakdown:

___% Splattered against the wall   ___% Eaten by my kid

___% Hidden in the napkin   ___% Other: _____

___% Fed to the dog   _____

Extra Mom Notes:

_____

_____

_____

_____

_____

_____

What's one thing my child did today that will embarrass him or her when he or she is a teenager?

_____

_____

Today's "Bad Mom" moment:

_____

_____

Today's "Best Mom Ever!" moment:

_____

_____

Based on my child's behavior today, I am sure he or she will grow up to be:

☐ A poet—so quiet and thoughtful!

☐ A boxer—so strong and tough!

☐ A political pundit—so loud and fussy!

☐ An Olympic sprinter—always on the go!

☐ A stand-up comedian—so funny and giggly!

☐ Other: _____ because _____

Extra Mom Notes:

_____

_____

_____

_____

_____

_____

_____

_____

Thursday

What's one lie I told my kid today? (That babies come from storks?
That all of the nutrients are in the bread's crust?)

_____

_____

If a TV camera crew followed me around all day, they'd be filming:

☐ A wacky family sitcom, like _Everybody Loves Raymond_ or
Modern Family.

☐ A complex workplace drama, like _Grey's Anatomy_ or _The Good Wife._

☐ A cheesy soap opera, like _Days of Our Lives_ or _General Hospital._

☐ A hyperactive talent contest, like _America's Got Talent_ or _So You
Think You Can Dance._

☐ Other: A _____ show, like
_____

The best actor to play my child would be _____,
because: _____

_____

Based on how I feel today, the best actress to play me would be
_____. She would be perfect because:

_____

_____

Extra Mom Notes:

_____

_____

_____

_____

_____

Friday Favorites!

My child's favorite toy this week was _____

This week, my child's favorite friend was _____

If I had to describe this friend in one word, it would be _____
If I had to describe this friend's parents in one word, it would be
_____

The song my child listened to the most this week was
_____

My feelings about this song:

☐ Love it—one of my favorites!
☐ Like it.
☐ Tolerate it—it could be worse, I guess.
☐ Annoyed by it—it's starting to get on my nerves.
☐ Loathe it—it makes my ears bleed.

The food my child asked for the most this week was _____

I ☐ did ☐ didn't give him or her this food because:
_____
_____

My favorite mom activity is _____ because:
_____
_____

Extra Mom Notes:
_____
_____
_____
_____

Saturday

Who was my parenting role model today? (Inspiration can come from anywhere, including your favorite TV character, your own parents, even the patient clerk at your local grocery store!)

_____

_____

If my child remembers one thing about today, I hope he or she remembers this:

_____

_____

Make Your Own Bedtime Story!

Once upon a time there was a _____ kid. That child had a mom who was really _____.

One day, the mom and the kid went on an adventure. First, they went to _____. There they met a big _____, who taught them both how to _____.

"_____!" said the kid. "This is the best _____ ever!"

Next, the mom and the kid went to _____. They played _____ and won!

"That was _____," said the mom, "but now let's go home."

So the mom and the kid went home and ate _____ for dinner.

They brushed their teeth, put on their _____, and went to bed.

Extra Mom Notes:

_____

_____

_____

_____

_____

Weekly Look Back

What's one thing that I learned about my child this week?

_____

_____

_____

What's one thing that my child learned about me this week?

_____

_____

_____

What's one thing that I learned about myself?

_____

_____

_____

What's my biggest hope for next week?

_____

_____

_____

Extra Mom Notes:

_____

_____

_____

_____

_____

_____

_____

_____

Monday

What was the cutest thing my child did today?

_____

_____

What did my kid smell like today? (Shampoo? Fruit punch? The family dog?)

_____

_____

What did I do today that I never would have done before I was a mom?

_____

_____

How much sleep did I get last night?

☐ More than 8 hours: I feel like a Disney princess!

☐ Between 6 and 8 hours: A few hits on the ol' snooze button, and I'm good to go.

☐ Between 3 and 6 hours: My face is permanently stuck in the yawn position.

☐ Between 1 and 3 hours: I now understand how zombies feel.

☐ Sleep? Hahaha! HAHAHAHA!

Extra Mom Notes:

_____

_____

_____

_____

_____

_____

DATE

The funniest thing my child did today was:

_____

_____

I ☐ did ☐ didn't laugh because:

_____

_____

What did I do today that made my child laugh?

_____

_____

If I could go back in time, what's one thing that I'd "do over" today?

_____

_____

Today I wished that I was my child's age so that I could

_____

_____ !

The mealtime breakdown:

___% Splattered against the wall   ___% Eaten by my kid

___% Hidden in the napkin   ___% Other: _____

___% Fed to the dog   _____

Extra Mom Notes:

_____

_____

_____

_____

_____

Wednesday

What's one thing my child did today that will embarrass him or her when he or she is a teenager?

_____

_____

Today's "Bad Mom" moment:

_____

_____

Today's "Best Mom Ever!" moment:

_____

_____

Based on my child's behavior today, I am sure he or she will grow up to be:

☐ A poet—so quiet and thoughtful!

☐ A boxer—so strong and tough!

☐ A political pundit—so loud and fussy!

☐ An Olympic sprinter—always on the go!

☐ A stand-up comedian—so funny and giggly!

☐ Other: _____ because _____

Extra Mom Notes:

_____

_____

_____

_____

_____

_____

_____

_____

What's one lie I told my kid today? (That babies come from storks? That all of the nutrients are in the bread's crust?)

_____

_____

If a TV camera crew followed me around all day, they'd be filming:

☐ A wacky family sitcom, like *Everybody Loves Raymond* or *Modern Family.*

☐ A complex workplace drama, like *Grey's Anatomy* or *The Good Wife.*

☐ A cheesy soap opera, like *Days of Our Lives* or *General Hospital.*

☐ A hyperactive talent contest, like *America's Got Talent* or *So You Think You Can Dance.*

☐ Other: A _____ show, like

_____

The best actor to play my child would be _____,

because: _____

_____

Based on how I feel today, the best actress to play me would be

_____. She would be perfect because:

_____

_____

Extra Mom Notes:

_____

_____

_____

_____

_____

Friday Favorites! DATE _____

My child's favorite toy this week was _____

This week, my child's favorite friend was _____

If I had to describe this friend in one word, it would be _____
If I had to describe this friend's parents in one word, it would be
_____

The song my child listened to the most this week was
_____

My feelings about this song:
☐ Love it—one of my favorites!
☐ Like it.
☐ Tolerate it—it could be worse, I guess.
☐ Annoyed by it—it's starting to get on my nerves.
☐ Loathe it—it makes my ears bleed.

The food my child asked for the most this week was _____

I ☐ did ☐ didn't give him or her this food because:
_____
_____

My favorite mom activity is _____ because:
_____
_____

Extra Mom Notes:
_____
_____
_____
_____

Saturday

Who was my parenting role model today? (Inspiration can come from anywhere, including your favorite TV character, your own parents, even the patient clerk at your local grocery store!)

_____

_____

If my child remembers one thing about today, I hope he or she remembers this:

_____

_____

Make Your Own Bedtime Story!

Once upon a time there was a _____ kid. That child had a mom who was really _____.

One day, the mom and the kid went on an adventure. First, they went to _____. There they met a big _____, who taught them both how to _____.

"_____!" said the kid. "This is the best _____ ever!"

Next, the mom and the kid went to _____. They played _____ and won!

"That was _____," said the mom, "but now let's go home."

So the mom and the kid went home and ate _____ for dinner. They brushed their teeth, put on their _____, and went to bed.

Extra Mom Notes:

_____

_____

_____

_____

_____

Sunday

Weekly Look Back

What's one thing that I learned about my child this week?

_____

_____

_____

What's one thing that my child learned about me this week?

_____

_____

_____

What's one thing that I learned about myself?

_____

_____

_____

What's my biggest hope for next week?

_____

_____

_____

Extra Mom Notes:

_____

_____

_____

_____

_____

_____

_____

What was the cutest thing my child did today?

_____
_____

What did my kid smell like today? (Shampoo? Fruit punch? The family dog?)

_____
_____

What did I do today that I never would have done before I was a mom?

_____
_____

How much sleep did I get last night?

☐ More than 8 hours: I feel like a Disney princess!

☐ Between 6 and 8 hours: A few hits on the ol' snooze button, and I'm good to go.

☐ Between 3 and 6 hours: My face is permanently stuck in the yawn position.

☐ Between 1 and 3 hours: I now understand how zombies feel.

☐ Sleep? Hahaha! HAHAHAHA!

Extra Mom Notes:

_____
_____
_____
_____
_____
_____
_____

Tuesday

The funniest thing my child did today was:

_____

_____

I ☐ did ☐ didn't laugh because:

_____

_____

What did I do today that made my child laugh?

_____

_____

If I could go back in time, what's one thing that I'd "do over" today?

_____

_____

Today I wished that I was my child's age so that I could

_____

_____!

The mealtime breakdown:

___% Splattered against the wall   ___% Eaten by my kid

___% Hidden in the napkin   ___% Other: _____

___% Fed to the dog   _____

Extra Mom Notes:

_____

_____

_____

_____

_____

_____

Wednesday

What's one thing my child did today that will embarrass him or her when he or she is a teenager?

_____

_____

Today's "Bad Mom" moment:

_____

_____

Today's "Best Mom Ever!" moment:

_____

_____

Based on my child's behavior today, I am sure he or she will grow up to be:

☐ A poet—so quiet and thoughtful!

☐ A boxer—so strong and tough!

☐ A political pundit—so loud and fussy!

☐ An Olympic sprinter—always on the go!

☐ A stand-up comedian—so funny and giggly!

☐ Other: _____ because _____

Extra Mom Notes:

_____

_____

_____

_____

_____

_____

_____

_____

Thursday

What's one lie I told my kid today? (That babies come from storks?
That all of the nutrients are in the bread's crust?)

_____

_____

If a TV camera crew followed me around all day, they'd be filming:

☐ A wacky family sitcom, like _Everybody Loves Raymond_ or
Modern Family.

☐ A complex workplace drama, like _Grey's Anatomy_ or _The Good Wife._

☐ A cheesy soap opera, like _Days of Our Lives_ or _General Hospital._

☐ A hyperactive talent contest, like _America's Got Talent_ or _So You
Think You Can Dance._

☐ Other: A _____ show, like

_____

The best actor to play my child would be _____,
because: _____

_____

Based on how I feel today, the best actress to play me would be
_____. She would be perfect because:

_____

_____

Extra Mom Notes:

_____

_____

_____

_____

_____

Friday Favorites!

My child's favorite toy this week was _____

This week, my child's favorite friend was _____

If I had to describe this friend in one word, it would be _____
If I had to describe this friend's parents in one word, it would be
_____

The song my child listened to the most this week was
_____

My feelings about this song:
- ☐ Love it—one of my favorites!
- ☐ Like it.
- ☐ Tolerate it—it could be worse, I guess.
- ☐ Annoyed by it—it's starting to get on my nerves.
- ☐ Loathe it—it makes my ears bleed.

The food my child asked for the most this week was _____

I ☐ did ☐ didn't give him or her this food because:
_____
_____

My favorite mom activity is _____ because:
_____
_____

Extra Mom Notes:
_____
_____
_____
_____

Saturday

Who was my parenting role model today? (Inspiration can come from anywhere, including your favorite TV character, your own parents, even the patient clerk at your local grocery store!)

_____

_____

If my child remembers one thing about today, I hope he or she remembers this:

_____

_____

Make Your Own Bedtime Story!

Once upon a time there was a _____ kid. That child had a mom who was really _____.

One day, the mom and the kid went on an adventure. First, they went to _____. There they met a big _____, who taught them both how to _____.

"_____!" said the kid. "This is the best _____ ever!"

Next, the mom and the kid went to _____. They played _____ and won!

"That was _____," said the mom, "but now let's go home."

So the mom and the kid went home and ate _____ for dinner. They brushed their teeth, put on their _____, and went to bed.

Extra Mom Notes:

_____

_____

_____

_____

_____

Weekly Look Back

What's one thing that I learned about my child this week?

_____
_____
_____

What's one thing that my child learned about me this week?

_____
_____
_____

What's one thing that I learned about myself?

_____
_____
_____

What's my biggest hope for next week?

_____
_____
_____

Extra Mom Notes:

_____
_____
_____
_____
_____
_____
_____

Monday

What was the cutest thing my child did today?

_____

_____

What did my kid smell like today? (Shampoo? Fruit punch?
The family dog?)

_____

_____

What did I do today that I never would have done before I was
a mom?

_____

_____

How much sleep did I get last night?

☐ More than 8 hours: I feel like a Disney princess!

☐ Between 6 and 8 hours: A few hits on the ol' snooze button, and
    I'm good to go.

☐ Between 3 and 6 hours: My face is permanently stuck in the yawn
    position.

☐ Between 1 and 3 hours: I now understand how zombies feel.

☐ Sleep? Hahaha! HAHAHAHA!

Extra Mom Notes:

_____

_____

_____

_____

_____

_____

_____

The funniest thing my child did today was:

_____

_____

I ☐ did ☐ didn't laugh because:

_____

_____

What did I do today that made my child laugh?

_____

_____

If I could go back in time, what's one thing that I'd "do over" today?

_____

_____

Today I wished that I was my child's age so that I could

_____

_____ !

The mealtime breakdown:

___% Splattered against the wall   ___% Eaten by my kid

___% Hidden in the napkin   ___% Other: _____

___% Fed to the dog   _____

Extra Mom Notes:

_____

_____

_____

_____

_____

Wednesday

What's one thing my child did today that will embarrass him or her when he or she is a teenager?

_____

_____

Today's "Bad Mom" moment:

_____

_____

Today's "Best Mom Ever!" moment:

_____

_____

Based on my child's behavior today, I am sure he or she will grow up to be:

☐ A poet—so quiet and thoughtful!

☐ A boxer—so strong and tough!

☐ A political pundit—so loud and fussy!

☐ An Olympic sprinter—always on the go!

☐ A stand-up comedian—so funny and giggly!

☐ Other: _____ because _____

Extra Mom Notes:

_____

_____

_____

_____

_____

_____

_____

_____

Thursday

What's one lie I told my kid today? (That babies come from storks? That all of the nutrients are in the bread's crust?)

_____

_____

If a TV camera crew followed me around all day, they'd be filming:

☐ A wacky family sitcom, like _Everybody Loves Raymond_ or _Modern Family_.

☐ A complex workplace drama, like _Grey's Anatomy_ or _The Good Wife_.

☐ A cheesy soap opera, like _Days of Our Lives_ or _General Hospital_.

☐ A hyperactive talent contest, like _America's Got Talent_ or _So You Think You Can Dance_.

☐ Other: A _____ show, like

_____

The best actor to play my child would be _____,

because: _____

_____

Based on how I feel today, the best actress to play me would be

_____. She would be perfect because:

_____

_____

Extra Mom Notes:

_____

_____

_____

_____

_____

Friday Favorites! DATE

My child's favorite toy this week was _____

This week, my child's favorite friend was _____

If I had to describe this friend in one word, it would be _____
If I had to describe this friend's parents in one word, it would be
_____

The song my child listened to the most this week was
_____

My feelings about this song:
☐ Love it—one of my favorites!
☐ Like it.
☐ Tolerate it—it could be worse, I guess.
☐ Annoyed by it—it's starting to get on my nerves.
☐ Loathe it—it makes my ears bleed.

The food my child asked for the most this week was _____

I ☐ did   ☐ didn't   give him or her this food because:
_____
_____

My favorite mom activity is _____ because:
_____
_____

Extra Mom Notes:
_____
_____
_____
_____

Who was my parenting role model today? (Inspiration can come from anywhere, including your favorite TV character, your own parents, even the patient clerk at your local grocery store!)

_____

_____

If my child remembers one thing about today, I hope he or she remembers this:

_____

_____

Make Your Own Bedtime Story!

Once upon a time there was a _____ kid. That child had a mom who was really _____.

One day, the mom and the kid went on an adventure. First, they went to _____. There they met a big _____, who taught them both how to _____.

"_____!" said the kid. "This is the best _____ ever!"

Next, the mom and the kid went to _____. They played _____ and won!

"That was _____," said the mom, "but now let's go home."

So the mom and the kid went home and ate _____ for dinner.

They brushed their teeth, put on their _____, and went to bed.

Extra Mom Notes:

_____

_____

_____

_____

_____

Sunday

DATE

Weekly Look Back

What's one thing that I learned about my child this week?

_____
_____
_____

What's one thing that my child learned about me this week?

_____
_____
_____

What's one thing that I learned about myself?

_____
_____
_____

What's my biggest hope for next week?

_____
_____
_____

Extra Mom Notes:

_____
_____
_____
_____
_____
_____
_____

What was the cutest thing my child did today?

_____

_____

What did my kid smell like today? (Shampoo? Fruit punch? The family dog?)

_____

_____

What did I do today that I never would have done before I was a mom?

_____

_____

How much sleep did I get last night?

☐ **More than 8 hours:** I feel like a Disney princess!

☐ **Between 6 and 8 hours:** A few hits on the ol' snooze button, and I'm good to go.

☐ **Between 3 and 6 hours:** My face is permanently stuck in the yawn position.

☐ **Between 1 and 3 hours:** I now understand how zombies feel.

☐ **Sleep?** Hahaha! HAHAHAHA!

Extra Mom Notes:

_____

_____

_____

_____

_____

_____

Tuesday

DATE

The funniest thing my child did today was:

_____

_____

I ☐ did ☐ didn't laugh because:

_____

_____

What did I do today that made my child laugh?

_____

_____

If I could go back in time, what's one thing that I'd "do over" today?

_____

_____

Today I wished that I was my child's age so that I could

_____

_____ !

The mealtime breakdown:

___% Splattered against the wall   ___% Eaten by my kid

___% Hidden in the napkin   ___% Other: _____

___% Fed to the dog   _____

Extra Mom Notes:

_____

_____

_____

_____

_____

What's one thing my child did today that will embarrass him or her when he or she is a teenager?

_____

_____

Today's "Bad Mom" moment:

_____

_____

Today's "Best Mom Ever!" moment:

_____

_____

Based on my child's behavior today, I am sure he or she will grow up to be:

☐ A poet—so quiet and thoughtful!

☐ A boxer—so strong and tough!

☐ A political pundit—so loud and fussy!

☐ An Olympic sprinter—always on the go!

☐ A stand-up comedian—so funny and giggly!

☐ Other: _____ because _____

Extra Mom Notes:

_____

_____

_____

_____

_____

_____

_____

Thursday

What's one lie I told my kid today? (That babies come from storks? That all of the nutrients are in the bread's crust?)

_____

_____

If a TV camera crew followed me around all day, they'd be filming:

☐ A wacky family sitcom, like _Everybody Loves Raymond_ or _Modern Family._

☐ A complex workplace drama, like _Grey's Anatomy_ or _The Good Wife._

☐ A cheesy soap opera, like _Days of Our Lives_ or _General Hospital._

☐ A hyperactive talent contest, like _America's Got Talent_ or _So You Think You Can Dance._

☐ Other: A _____ show, like

_____

The best actor to play my child would be _____,

because: _____

_____

Based on how I feel today, the best actress to play me would be

_____. She would be perfect because:

_____

_____

Extra Mom Notes:

_____

_____

_____

_____

_____

Friday Favorites!

My child's favorite toy this week was _____

This week, my child's favorite friend was _____

If I had to describe this friend in one word, it would be _____
If I had to describe this friend's parents in one word, it would be
_____

The song my child listened to the most this week was
_____

My feelings about this song:

☐ Love it—one of my favorites!
☐ Like it.
☐ Tolerate it—it could be worse, I guess.
☐ Annoyed by it—it's starting to get on my nerves.
☐ Loathe it—it makes my ears bleed.

The food my child asked for the most this week was _____

I ☐ did ☐ didn't give him or her this food because:
_____
_____

My favorite mom activity is _____ because:
_____
_____

Extra Mom Notes:
_____
_____
_____
_____

Saturday

Who was my parenting role model today? (Inspiration can come from anywhere, including your favorite TV character, your own parents, even the patient clerk at your local grocery store!)

_____

_____

If my child remembers one thing about today, I hope he or she remembers this:

_____

_____

Make Your Own Bedtime Story!

Once upon a time there was a _____ kid. That child had a mom who was really _____.

One day, the mom and the kid went on an adventure. First, they went to _____. There they met a big _____, who taught them both how to _____.

"_____!" said the kid. "This is the best _____ ever!" Next, the mom and the kid went to _____. They played _____ and won!

"That was _____," said the mom, "but now let's go home." So the mom and the kid went home and ate _____ for dinner. They brushed their teeth, put on their _____, and went to bed.

Extra Mom Notes:

_____

_____

_____

_____

_____

Weekly Look Back

What's one thing that I learned about my child this week?

_____
_____
_____

What's one thing that my child learned about me this week?

_____
_____
_____

What's one thing that I learned about myself?

_____
_____
_____

What's my biggest hope for next week?

_____
_____
_____

Extra Mom Notes:

_____
_____
_____
_____
_____
_____
_____
_____

Monday

What was the cutest thing my child did today?

_____

_____

What did my kid smell like today? (Shampoo? Fruit punch? The family dog?)

_____

_____

What did I do today that I never would have done before I was a mom?

_____

_____

How much sleep did I get last night?

☐ More than 8 hours: I feel like a Disney princess!

☐ Between 6 and 8 hours: A few hits on the ol' snooze button, and I'm good to go.

☐ Between 3 and 6 hours: My face is permanently stuck in the yawn position.

☐ Between 1 and 3 hours: I now understand how zombies feel.

☐ Sleep? Hahaha! HAHAHAHA!

Extra Mom Notes:

_____

_____

_____

_____

_____

_____

DATE

The funniest thing my child did today was:

_____

_____

I ☐ did ☐ didn't laugh because:

_____

_____

What did I do today that made my child laugh?

_____

_____

If I could go back in time, what's one thing that I'd "do over" today?

_____

_____

Today I wished that I was my child's age so that I could

_____

_____ !

The mealtime breakdown:

___% Splattered against the wall   ___% Eaten by my kid

___% Hidden in the napkin   ___% Other: _____

___% Fed to the dog   _____

Extra Mom Notes:

_____

_____

_____

_____

_____

Wednesday

What's one thing my child did today that will embarrass him or her when he or she is a teenager?

_____
_____

Today's "Bad Mom" moment:

_____
_____

Today's "Best Mom Ever!" moment:

_____
_____

Based on my child's behavior today, I am sure he or she will grow up to be:

☐ A poet—so quiet and thoughtful!

☐ A boxer—so strong and tough!

☐ A political pundit—so loud and fussy!

☐ An Olympic sprinter—always on the go!

☐ A stand-up comedian—so funny and giggly!

☐ Other: _____ because _____

Extra Mom Notes:

_____
_____
_____
_____
_____
_____
_____
_____

Thursday

What's one lie I told my kid today? (That babies come from storks? That all of the nutrients are in the bread's crust?)

_____

_____

If a TV camera crew followed me around all day, they'd be filming:

☐ A wacky family sitcom, like *Everybody Loves Raymond* or *Modern Family*.

☐ A complex workplace drama, like *Grey's Anatomy* or *The Good Wife*.

☐ A cheesy soap opera, like *Days of Our Lives* or *General Hospital*.

☐ A hyperactive talent contest, like *America's Got Talent* or *So You Think You Can Dance*.

☐ Other: A _____ show, like

_____

The best actor to play my child would be _____,
because: _____

_____

Based on how I feel today, the best actress to play me would be
_____. She would be perfect because:

_____

_____

Extra Mom Notes:

_____

_____

_____

_____

_____

Friday Favorites! DATE

My child's favorite toy this week was _____

This week, my child's favorite friend was _____

If I had to describe this friend in one word, it would be _____
If I had to describe this friend's parents in one word, it would be
_____

The song my child listened to the most this week was
_____

My feelings about this song:
- ☐ Love it—one of my favorites!
- ☐ Like it.
- ☐ Tolerate it—it could be worse, I guess.
- ☐ Annoyed by it—it's starting to get on my nerves.
- ☐ Loathe it—it makes my ears bleed.

The food my child asked for the most this week was _____

I ☐ did ☐ didn't   give him or her this food because:
_____
_____

My favorite mom activity is _____ because:
_____
_____

Extra Mom Notes:
_____
_____
_____
_____

Saturday

Who was my parenting role model today? (Inspiration can come from anywhere, including your favorite TV character, your own parents, even the patient clerk at your local grocery store!)

_____

_____

If my child remembers one thing about today, I hope he or she remembers this:

_____

_____

Make Your Own Bedtime Story!

Once upon a time there was a _____ kid. That child had a mom who was really _____.

One day, the mom and the kid went on an adventure. First, they went to _____. There they met a big _____, who taught them both how to _____.

"_____!" said the kid. "This is the best _____ ever!"

Next, the mom and the kid went to _____. They played _____ and won!

"That was _____," said the mom, "but now let's go home."

So the mom and the kid went home and ate _____ for dinner. They brushed their teeth, put on their _____, and went to bed.

Extra Mom Notes:

_____

_____

_____

_____

_____

Sunday

Weekly Look Back

What's one thing that I learned about my child this week?

_____
_____
_____

What's one thing that my child learned about me this week?

_____
_____
_____

What's one thing that I learned about myself?

_____
_____
_____

What's my biggest hope for next week?

_____
_____
_____

Extra Mom Notes:

_____
_____
_____
_____
_____
_____
_____

Monday

What was the cutest thing my child did today?

_____

_____

What did my kid smell like today? (Shampoo? Fruit punch? The family dog?)

_____

_____

What did I do today that I never would have done before I was a mom?

_____

_____

How much sleep did I get last night?

☐ **More than 8 hours:** I feel like a Disney princess!

☐ **Between 6 and 8 hours:** A few hits on the ol' snooze button, and I'm good to go.

☐ **Between 3 and 6 hours:** My face is permanently stuck in the yawn position.

☐ **Between 1 and 3 hours:** I now understand how zombies feel.

☐ **Sleep?** Hahaha! HAHAHAHA!

Extra Mom Notes:

_____

_____

_____

_____

_____

_____

Tuesday

The funniest thing my child did today was:

_____

_____

I ☐ did ☐ didn't laugh because:

_____

_____

What did I do today that made my child laugh?

_____

_____

If I could go back in time, what's one thing that I'd "do over" today?

_____

_____

Today I wished that I was my child's age so that I could

_____

_____!

The mealtime breakdown:

___% Splattered against the wall   ___% Eaten by my kid

___% Hidden in the napkin   ___% Other: _____

___% Fed to the dog   _____

Extra Mom Notes:

_____

_____

_____

_____

_____

Wednesday

What's one thing my child did today that will embarrass him or her when he or she is a teenager?

_____

_____

Today's "Bad Mom" moment:

_____

_____

Today's "Best Mom Ever!" moment:

_____

_____

Based on my child's behavior today, I am sure he or she will grow up to be:

☐ A poet—so quiet and thoughtful!

☐ A boxer—so strong and tough!

☐ A political pundit—so loud and fussy!

☐ An Olympic sprinter—always on the go!

☐ A stand-up comedian—so funny and giggly!

☐ Other: _____ because _____

Extra Mom Notes:

_____

_____

_____

_____

_____

_____

_____

_____

Thursday

What's one lie I told my kid today? (That babies come from storks?
That all of the nutrients are in the bread's crust?)

_____

_____

If a TV camera crew followed me around all day, they'd be filming:

☐ A wacky family sitcom, like _Everybody Loves Raymond_ or
Modern Family.

☐ A complex workplace drama, like _Grey's Anatomy_ or _The Good Wife._

☐ A cheesy soap opera, like _Days of Our Lives_ or _General Hospital._

☐ A hyperactive talent contest, like _America's Got Talent_ or _So You
Think You Can Dance._

☐ Other: A _____ show, like

_____

The best actor to play my child would be _____,
because: _____

_____

Based on how I feel today, the best actress to play me would be
_____. She would be perfect because:

_____

_____

Extra Mom Notes:

_____

_____

_____

_____

_____

Friday Favorites!

My child's favorite toy this week was _____

This week, my child's favorite friend was _____

If I had to describe this friend in one word, it would be _____
If I had to describe this friend's parents in one word, it would be
_____

The song my child listened to the most this week was
_____

My feelings about this song:
☐ Love it—one of my favorites!
☐ Like it.
☐ Tolerate it—it could be worse, I guess.
☐ Annoyed by it—it's starting to get on my nerves.
☐ Loathe it—it makes my ears bleed.

The food my child asked for the most this week was _____

I ☐ did ☐ didn't give him or her this food because:
_____
_____

My favorite mom activity is _____ because:
_____
_____

Extra Mom Notes:
_____
_____
_____
_____

Saturday

Who was my parenting role model today? (Inspiration can come from anywhere, including your favorite TV character, your own parents, even the patient clerk at your local grocery store!)

_____

_____

If my child remembers one thing about today, I hope he or she remembers this:

_____

_____

Make Your Own Bedtime Story!

Once upon a time there was a _____ kid. That child had a mom who was really _____.

One day, the mom and the kid went on an adventure. First, they went to _____. There they met a big _____, who taught them both how to _____.

"_____!" said the kid. "This is the best _____ ever!"

Next, the mom and the kid went to _____. They played _____ and won!

"That was _____," said the mom, "but now let's go home."

So the mom and the kid went home and ate _____ for dinner.

They brushed their teeth, put on their _____, and went to bed.

Extra Mom Notes:

_____

_____

_____

_____

_____

Sunday

Weekly Look Back

What's one thing that I learned about my child this week?

_____
_____
_____

What's one thing that my child learned about me this week?

_____
_____
_____

What's one thing that I learned about myself?

_____
_____
_____

What's my biggest hope for next week?

_____
_____
_____

Extra Mom Notes:

_____
_____
_____
_____
_____
_____
_____

Monday

What was the cutest thing my child did today?

_____

_____

What did my kid smell like today? (Shampoo? Fruit punch? The family dog?)

_____

_____

What did I do today that I never would have done before I was a mom?

_____

_____

How much sleep did I get last night?

☐ More than 8 hours: I feel like a Disney princess!

☐ Between 6 and 8 hours: A few hits on the ol' snooze button, and I'm good to go.

☐ Between 3 and 6 hours: My face is permanently stuck in the yawn position.

☐ Between 1 and 3 hours: I now understand how zombies feel.

☐ Sleep? Hahaha! HAHAHAHA!

Extra Mom Notes:

_____

_____

_____

_____

_____

_____

_____

The funniest thing my child did today was:

_____

_____

I ☐ did ☐ didn't laugh because:

_____

_____

What did I do today that made my child laugh?

_____

_____

If I could go back in time, what's one thing that I'd "do over" today?

_____

_____

Today I wished that I was my child's age so that I could

_____

_____!

The mealtime breakdown:

___% Splattered against the wall   ___% Eaten by my kid

___% Hidden in the napkin   ___% Other: _____

___% Fed to the dog   _____

Extra Mom Notes:

_____

_____

_____

_____

_____

Wednesday

What's one thing my child did today that will embarrass him or her when he or she is a teenager?

_____

_____

Today's "Bad Mom" moment:

_____

_____

Today's "Best Mom Ever!" moment:

_____

_____

Based on my child's behavior today, I am sure he or she will grow up to be:

☐ A poet—so quiet and thoughtful!

☐ A boxer—so strong and tough!

☐ A political pundit—so loud and fussy!

☐ An Olympic sprinter—always on the go!

☐ A stand-up comedian—so funny and giggly!

☐ Other: _____ because _____

Extra Mom Notes:

_____

_____

_____

_____

_____

_____

_____

_____

Thursday

What's one lie I told my kid today? (That babies come from storks? That all of the nutrients are in the bread's crust?)

_____

_____

If a TV camera crew followed me around all day, they'd be filming:

☐ A wacky family sitcom, like _Everybody Loves Raymond_ or _Modern Family._

☐ A complex workplace drama, like _Grey's Anatomy_ or _The Good Wife._

☐ A cheesy soap opera, like _Days of Our Lives_ or _General Hospital._

☐ A hyperactive talent contest, like _America's Got Talent_ or _So You Think You Can Dance._

☐ Other: A _____ show, like

_____

The best actor to play my child would be _____,
because: _____

_____

Based on how I feel today, the best actress to play me would be
_____. She would be perfect because:

_____

_____

Extra Mom Notes:

_____

_____

_____

_____

_____

Friday Favorites! DATE

My child's favorite toy this week was _____

This week, my child's favorite friend was _____

If I had to describe this friend in one word, it would be _____
If I had to describe this friend's parents in one word, it would be
_____

The song my child listened to the most this week was
_____

My feelings about this song:
☐ Love it—one of my favorites!
☐ Like it.
☐ Tolerate it—it could be worse, I guess.
☐ Annoyed by it—it's starting to get on my nerves.
☐ Loathe it—it makes my ears bleed.

The food my child asked for the most this week was _____

I ☐ did ☐ didn't give him or her this food because:
_____
_____

My favorite mom activity is _____ because:
_____
_____

Extra Mom Notes:
_____
_____
_____
_____

Who was my parenting role model today? (Inspiration can come from anywhere, including your favorite TV character, your own parents, even the patient clerk at your local grocery store!)

_____

_____

If my child remembers one thing about today, I hope he or she remembers this:

_____

_____

Make Your Own Bedtime Story!

Once upon a time there was a _____ kid. That child had a mom who was really _____.

One day, the mom and the kid went on an adventure. First, they went to _____. There they met a big _____, who taught them both how to _____.

"_____!" said the kid. "This is the best _____ ever!"

Next, the mom and the kid went to _____. They played _____ and won!

"That was _____," said the mom, "but now let's go home."

So the mom and the kid went home and ate _____ for dinner.

They brushed their teeth, put on their _____, and went to bed.

Extra Mom Notes:

_____

_____

_____

_____

_____

Sunday

Weekly Look Back

What's one thing that I learned about my child this week?

_____

_____

_____

What's one thing that my child learned about me this week?

_____

_____

_____

What's one thing that I learned about myself?

_____

_____

_____

What's my biggest hope for next week?

_____

_____

_____

Extra Mom Notes:

_____

_____

_____

_____

_____

_____

_____

What was the cutest thing my child did today?

_____

_____

What did my kid smell like today? (Shampoo? Fruit punch? The family dog?)

_____

_____

What did I do today that I never would have done before I was a mom?

_____

_____

How much sleep did I get last night?

☐ More than 8 hours: I feel like a Disney princess!

☐ Between 6 and 8 hours: A few hits on the ol' snooze button, and I'm good to go.

☐ Between 3 and 6 hours: My face is permanently stuck in the yawn position.

☐ Between 1 and 3 hours: I now understand how zombies feel.

☐ Sleep? Hahaha! HAHAHAHA!

Extra Mom Notes:

_____

_____

_____

_____

_____

_____

Tuesday

The funniest thing my child did today was:

_____

_____

I ☐ did ☐ didn't laugh because:

_____

_____

What did I do today that made my child laugh?

_____

_____

If I could go back in time, what's one thing that I'd "do over" today?

_____

_____

Today I wished that I was my child's age so that I could

_____

_____ !

The mealtime breakdown:

___% Splattered against the wall   ___% Eaten by my kid

___% Hidden in the napkin   ___% Other: _____

___% Fed to the dog   _____

Extra Mom Notes:

_____

_____

_____

_____

_____

_____

What's one thing my child did today that will embarrass him or her when he or she is a teenager?

_____

_____

Today's "Bad Mom" moment:

_____

_____

Today's "Best Mom Ever!" moment:

_____

_____

Based on my child's behavior today, I am sure he or she will grow up to be:

☐ A poet—so quiet and thoughtful!

☐ A boxer—so strong and tough!

☐ A political pundit—so loud and fussy!

☐ An Olympic sprinter—always on the go!

☐ A stand-up comedian—so funny and giggly!

☐ Other: _____ because _____

Extra Mom Notes:

_____

_____

_____

_____

_____

_____

_____

_____

Thursday

What's one lie I told my kid today? (That babies come from storks? That all of the nutrients are in the bread's crust?)

_____

_____

If a TV camera crew followed me around all day, they'd be filming:

☐ A wacky family sitcom, like _Everybody Loves Raymond_ or _Modern Family._

☐ A complex workplace drama, like _Grey's Anatomy_ or _The Good Wife._

☐ A cheesy soap opera, like _Days of Our Lives_ or _General Hospital._

☐ A hyperactive talent contest, like _America's Got Talent_ or _So You Think You Can Dance._

☐ Other: A _____ show, like

_____

The best actor to play my child would be _____,
because: _____

_____

Based on how I feel today, the best actress to play me would be
_____. She would be perfect because:

_____

_____

Extra Mom Notes:

_____

_____

_____

_____

_____

Friday Favorites!

My child's favorite toy this week was _____

This week, my child's favorite friend was _____

If I had to describe this friend in one word, it would be _____
If I had to describe this friend's parents in one word, it would be
_____

The song my child listened to the most this week was
_____

My feelings about this song:
☐ Love it—one of my favorites!
☐ Like it.
☐ Tolerate it—it could be worse, I guess.
☐ Annoyed by it—it's starting to get on my nerves.
☐ Loathe it—it makes my ears bleed.

The food my child asked for the most this week was _____

I ☐ did ☐ didn't **give him or her this food because:**
_____
_____

My favorite mom activity is _____ **because:**
_____
_____

Extra Mom Notes:
_____
_____
_____
_____

Saturday

\boxed{\text{DATE}}

Who was my parenting role model today? (Inspiration can come from anywhere, including your favorite TV character, your own parents, even the patient clerk at your local grocery store!)

_____

_____

If my child remembers one thing about today, I hope he or she remembers this:

_____

_____

Make Your Own Bedtime Story!

Once upon a time there was a _____ kid. That child had a mom who was really _____.

One day, the mom and the kid went on an adventure. First, they went to _____. There they met a big _____, who taught them both how to _____.

"_____!" said the kid. "This is the best _____ ever!"

Next, the mom and the kid went to _____. They played _____ and won!

"That was _____," said the mom, "but now let's go home."

So the mom and the kid went home and ate _____ for dinner. They brushed their teeth, put on their _____, and went to bed.

Extra Mom Notes:

_____

_____

_____

_____

_____

Weekly Look Back

What's one thing that I learned about my child this week?

_____

_____

_____

What's one thing that my child learned about me this week?

_____

_____

_____

What's one thing that I learned about myself?

_____

_____

_____

What's my biggest hope for next week?

_____

_____

_____

Extra Mom Notes:

_____

_____

_____

_____

_____

_____

_____